TYNE & WEAR

Edited by Allison Dowse

First published in Great Britain in 2003 by
YOUNG WRITERS
Remus House,
Coltsfoot Drive,
Peterborough, PE2 9JX
Telephone (01733) 890066

All Rights Reserved

Copyright Contributors 2003

HB ISBN 0 75434 231 X
SB ISBN 0 75434 232 8

FOREWORD

This year, the Young Writers' The Write Stuff! competition proudly presents a showcase of the best poetic talent from over 40,000 up-and-coming writers nationwide.

Young Writers was established in 1991 and we are still successful, even in today's modern world, in promoting and encouraging the reading and writing of poetry.

The thought, effort, imagination and hard work put into each poem impressed us all, and once again, the task of selecting poems was a difficult one, but nevertheless, an enjoyable experience.

We hope you are as pleased as we are with the final selection and that you and your family continue to be entertained with *The Write Stuff! Tyne & Wear* for many years to come.

Contents

Collingwood School
- Kim Barrass — 1
- Sarah Hope — 1
- Ruth Harrison — 2

Hebburn Comprehensive School
- Ashleigh Flaherty — 2
- Andrew Thornton — 2
- Kristofer Gibson — 3
- Laura Crompton — 3
- Charlotte Allen — 3
- Avril Lagan — 4
- Natasha Taylor — 4
- Rebecca English — 4
- Chanelle Fowlie — 5
- Jade Williamson — 6

Hookergate School
- Melissa Nichol — 6
- Marie Chapman — 7
- Thomas Wilson — 7
- Sarah Forster — 8
- Harriet Corrighan — 8
- Lindsay Herron — 9
- Stuart Chapman — 10
- Sarah Hynes — 10
- Zoe Snaith — 11
- Robert Hawley — 12
- Cheryl Anderson — 12
- Carly Hope — 13
- Ryan Welsh — 14
- Terri Adamson — 15
- Catherine Colesby — 16
- Christopher Dodd — 16
- Anthony McConnell — 17
- Liam Nichol — 17

Beth Atkinson	18
Ami Riddell	19
Ashleigh Gibson	20
Sophie Wardhaugh	21
Christopher Kane	22
Lucretia Nolan	22
Laura Teasdale	23
Ginna Ord	23
Victoria Johnson	24
Christopher Wilkinson	24
Vincent Tsang	25
Laura Simmonds	26
Mark True	26
Carl Robinson	27
Kim Pattinson	28
Jill Shepherd	28
Ashleigh Hetherington	29
Sarah Young	29
Vicki Manning	30
Sam Gardner Little	30
Daniel Park	31
Craig Wilson	31
Scott Murray	32
Jade Hall	32
Laura Brown	33
Hannah Lefevre	33
Andrew Dixon	34
Sarah Bennett	35
Margaret Bell	36
Danielle Lowe	37
Sophie Scott	38
Stuart Bennett	39
Nicola Kirby	40
Guy Kelly	40
Ruth McKie	41
Danielle Morland	42
Steven Banks	42
Lynsey Halliday	43

Jasmine Grey	44
Charlotte Graham	44
Victoria Adams	45
Ashleigh Tiplady	45

Kenton School

Joseph Edward Grugeon-Dixon	46
Jason Rudowski	46
Matthew Dunn	47
Robert Carver	48
Samantha Shiel	48
Dean Baxter	49
James Moore	50
Amir Asghari	50
Kaylie Mulholland	51
Kayleigh Balmer	52
Matthew Lee	52

Ponteland County High School

Deile Turnbull	53
Adam Soulsby	53
Nikki Gilbertson	54
Sarah Duggan	54
Kate Wallis	55
James Fisher	55
Jay Mihcioglu	56
Adam Houghton	56
Danielle Blacklock	56
David Collis	57
Garry Wilson	57
Andrew Hayes	58
Nicholas Mathieson	58
Ryan Johnson	58
Amy Daley	59
Sam Taylor	59
Adam McEnaney	59
John Thomson	60
Michael Carr	60

Holly Lillico	60
Alex Sandercock	61
Sarah Duffy	61
Alison Holmes	61
Danielle Hawkins	62
Lindsey Willis	62

Usworth Comprehensive School

Craig Hodgson	63
David Smith	63
Lee Atkinson	64
Jemma Burton	64
Sophie Minnis	65
Chelsey Taylor	65
Kayleigh Abbott	66
Christopher James French	66
Louise Donkin	67
Claire Reid	67
Nicola Bain	68
Carley Lawrence	68
Chris Davies	69
Zoe Bell	69
Laura Handy	70
Sean Herron	70
Cheryl Robinson	71
Ashleigh Ord	71
Alexandra Muter	72
Ryan Ellis	72
Lindsay Purvis	73
Laura Rackstraw	73
Stephanie Johnson	74
Charlotte Walton	74
Gemma Horn	74
Ashleigh Lupton	75
Lee Ridley	75
Danny Needham	76
Sarah Rossiter	76
Mark King	77

Nick Shotton	78
Vicky Mason	78
Harry Robson	79
Dean King	79
Brent Johnson	80
Dee Robson	80
Karl Horn	80
Emma Naisby	81
Samantha Wallace	81
Sophie Parish	82
Mark Tulip	82
Joanne Meikle	82
Rebecca Rowntree	83

Whitburn School

Marcus Javan	83
Laura Kirk	84
John Romans	84
Jonathon Phinn	85
Matthew Ball	85
Mellisa Sanders	86
Lucy Walker	86
Emma Naughton	87
Ryan Dent	87
Jonathan Dixon	88
Gavin Graham	88
Imogen Nicholson	89
Emma Landsbury	90
Liam Bruce	90
Stacey Banks	91
Amy Edmondson	91
Laura Stephenson	92
Peter Collinson	92
Tonya Robson	93
Christopher Lester	94
Gavin Haswell	94
Natasha Curry	95
Oliver Routledge	96

Ben Ball	96
Lloyd Humphrey	97
Kane Grant	97
Josh Gray	98
Graeme Jones	98
Rebecca Ross	99
Adam Shaw	100
Lee Brennan	101
Kay Rooney	102
Jennifer Preston	103
Daryl Hall	104
Kevin Hodgson	104
Stephen Guthrie	105
Lauren Ball	106
Nikita Mae Young	107
Alice Barnes	108
Hayley Conway	109
Reece Finch	110
Stephanie Urwin	110
Laura Ferry	111
Laurie Slesser	112
Joe Harrison	112
Jack Blythe	113
Isra Gabal	114
Daniel Gollagly	114
Stephanie McGuire	115
Gary Moon	116
Kieron McKay	116
Rebecca Turner	117
Verity Graham	117
Chris Glancey	118
Christa Archer	118
Mark Hamblett	119
Robert Jones	120
Julie Whitfield	120
Nathan Potter	121
Sam Harwood	122
Callum Watson	122

Luke Golding	123
Emma Mossavi	124
Emily Shields	125
Thomas Crutwell	126
Daniel Pye	126
Helen Thornton	127
Chris Kear	127
Daniel Callan	128
Louise Bailey	128
Antony Dorothy	129
Alex Nicol	129
Chris Furness	130
Craig Todd	131
Michael Brookes	132
Bethany Hammonds	132
Graham Burn	133
Daniel Fishwick	134
Claire Robson	134
Sarah Nicholson	135
Matthew Woodhouse	136
Steven Rutter	137
Sean Wakefield	138
Cameron Walker	139
Emma Irvine	140
Zoe Muse	141
Jamie Anderson	142
Jonathon McCulley	142
Christopher James Gardner	143
Vicki Midlane	144
Emmy Campbell	144
Lauren Jackson	145
Anthony Dunn	146
Amy Overton	147
Lauren Wilkinson	148
Laura Handy	149
Anna Carter	150
Laura Wilkinson	151
Stefanie Ford	152

Craig Young	152
Vanessa Curry	153
Andrew Clark	154
Johnathon Tulip	154
Sam Keane	155
Jamie Harding	156
Laura Fielding	156
Faye Buckingham	157
Victoria White	158
Michael Gowland	158

The Poems

REFLECTIONS

The sky is blue
The sky is bright
Sun shines in the sky
Clouds are white as snow
The wind blows cool and breezy
Rain drops like tears down your face
Snow gently falls to the ground
As we welcome winter.

Wrap up warm
Sit by the fire
Sip a hot chocolate
Feel a warm glow
Watch the rain and snow
Go to sleep and dream
About tomorrow.

Kim Barrass (16)
Collingwood School

SUN BRIGHT

Sun bright as a jewel
Shining in the sky
Blinding me as I walk by.
Sun was so bright I was getting too hot.
Sun was blocking my eye sight.
I couldn't see where I was going.
I went in the shade and sat down.
Blinking and looking for light.
Now the sun wasn't blocking my eyes
Everything was clear.

Sarah Hope (15)
Collingwood School

RAIN, RAIN ON THE GROUND

Rain, rain on the ground,
listen to the gentle sound
children playing on the yard
noise of a whistle blowing
cars move along the road
children fall into lines.

Ruth Harrison (15)
Collingwood School

THE CALLING

I see the dark navy sky through a cracked window,
I touched my face with a web and a spider crawled,
I taste the disgusting polluted sea air,
I smell the rotting animals and the darkness of the night,
I hear the poltergeist chanting as they come closer
                        and closer towards me!

Ashleigh Flaherty
Hebburn Comprehensive School

MY SENSES

I smell the erotic red roses in the garden.
I see the bright shine of the sun.
I hear the blue roaring ocean.
I taste the bitter salt of the sea.
I feel the soft smooth flowers touching my skin.

Andrew Thornton (12)
Hebburn Comprehensive School

I SEE THE BLUE WAVY SEA

I see the blue wavy sea.
I hear the sea splashing against the motionless grey rocks.
I taste the sweets that are being eaten by the vigorous children.
I smell the salty sea air and seaweed.
I touch the warm bristly sand of the misty seashore.

Kristofer Gibson
Hebburn Comprehensive School

THE UNKNOWN HOUSE

I see a wounded seagull through a shattered window
flying over the sea,
I feel a large spider cross my cheek and I start to quiver.
I smell the dampness of the cracked walls as I slowly walk
along the long corridor,
I have a sudden taste of polluted sea air in my mouth,
I hear the restless waves crashing against the high jagged cliffs,
as I leave the unknown house.

Laura Crompton (12)
Hebburn Comprehensive School

EXPLORING THE GARDEN!

I see the long, green, wavy grass blowing around.
I hear the birds chirping as they sit in their nest.
I taste the fresh air.
I touch the daffodils as a petal is blown off by the blustery wind.
I smell the pollen as it brushes past my nose.

Charlotte Allen
Hebburn Comprehensive School

WHISPERS IN THE MOONLIGHT

I see the murky shadows cast by the light of the silver moon,
I hear their mystical voices,
I taste the bitterness of the air around me,
I smell the harmonious flowers as I walk through the garden,
I feel the snatching branches of the trees clutching my hair,
as the whispers draw nearer,
then I turn the corner and suddenly the whispers stop.

Avril Lagan (13)
Hebburn Comprehensive School

THE GARDEN OF GLOOM

I saw the demolished sculpture lying in smithereens on
                                 the jagged gravel.
I heard the shrill cries of the falcon as it swooped down on its prey.
I felt the frost tingling rapidly up my spine.
I smelt the putrid stench of the decaying bird left by the falcon.
I tasted the nectar in the shrivelled flowers.

Natasha Taylor
Hebburn Comprehensive School

WINTER IS COMING

Winter is the greatest, with the snow and the hummingbirds.
The children playing and talking with their own silly little words.

        Winter is nearly here,
           It's coming,
           It's coming.

Christmas is approaching us with the sparkling snow,
The parents sitting in a sledge on a hill
Which is steep and very low.

Winter is nearly here,
It's coming,
It's coming.

Enjoy the winter.

Rebecca English (11)
Hebburn Comprehensive School

AUTUMN BEGINS

When the autumn weather begins to appear
it's very cold and damp out there.
When the wind blows in the sky
it blows the leaves all up high.
When the rain falls hard and fast
it makes you think of summer past.
When the frost begins to show
now you know it's time for snow.
When the snow hits the ground
it does not make any sound.

Autumn leaves are falling
the birds are calling.
The leaves lie on the ground
making their rustling sound.
They cover the lawns, paths and roads
my oh my, there're loads.
The leaves are turning brown
they're all over town.

As the dark nights creep in once more
it's time for carol singers to knock on the door.
They sing their Christmas songs
I can hear the church bells ding-dong.

Chanelle Fowlie (11)
Hebburn Comprehensive School

HEAVEN

I see the gleaming reflection of the golden sun,
I hear cheeping and chattering birds upon the towering trees,
I taste the pollen streaming out of the blooming flowers,
I smell the sweet fruit dangling from the apple trees,
I touch the sleek fur of an urban fox.

Jade Williamson
Hebburn Comprehensive School

WHY THIS?

Dressed in weeds.
In a pond.
A girl.
Alive or dead?
Floating down a pond or river.
She's thinking, *where am I?*
What will happen to me?
It is dark and cold.
Weeds and trees covering her like curtains.
She cannot move as the current takes her away.
She wants to get up and go home.
How did she get there?
Her life was always filled with happy things.
She has nothing left.
Nothing to live for anymore,
Looking up at the sky.
What is left for her now?

Melissa Nichol (12)
Hookergate School

MY CLASS

The first day in Year Six,
It really makes me feel sick,
But now I know
It's not so bad,
But some of the boys
Make me sad.
Sometimes the girls are OK
But they go away.
Our teacher Mrs Fisher
Likes to drink bitter.
As the day goes by
I realise that I am not so shy!

Marie Chapman (12)
Hookergate School

THE SUNFLOWER

In the midst of the morning dew lay upon the grass,
Birds sang in the morning breeze,
A single twig falls from the treetops,
A sunflower, tall, dazzling, there it was all alone,
It reached towards the sun with its cheerful face,
His leafy arms outstretched and his thin body twisted from head to toe,
Taller than the world he stands, a view of all the landscape,
A child playing far away,
A church bell ringing summons those who still believe,
And as twilight shadows his face, the sunflower holds his head high,
Ready for another day of tranquillity and majestic solitude.

Thomas Wilson (11)
Hookergate School

OPHELIA

Let her lie in a cold, dusty place.
Let her lie underneath the grass, that looks like swords.
The trees are blowing like the wind
With the leaves falling on her face.
She's lying with the leaves
And lets the bees fly around her.
Let her lie in the dark with animals coming and going.
Let her lie with the water running over her.
Let her ask a question, 'How did I get here?'
She thinks and thinks but no good.
So let her lie in the cold
Let her lie dying in the cold,
Let her shout, 'Help, help.'
Let her tears run down her face
With a dip in the water.
Let her listen to the birds calling her name.
The wind is getting stronger
And she is flowing downstream,
Where nobody knows where she's at.

Sarah Forster (13)
Hookergate School

THE BLOOD-RED ROSE

The blood-red rose, pricked me sharply on the hand,
What have I ever done to it? I don't understand,
I've never been unkind to it, I've just let it be,
So why has it been so spiteful, by hurting gentle me?

The blood-red rose, beside the garden wall,
I only tried to pick up my little bouncy ball,
I yelled out loud as it dug into my skin,
Gardener Jack came running to see what was the din.

The blood-red rose hurt old Gardener Jack,
He got very angry and gave it a whack,
It flew over the fence and hit off the floor,
Lost all its thorns, so it's prickly no more.

Harriet Corrighan (13)
Hookergate School

DEATH IN THE LAKE

There was a death in the lake.
A girl I saw.
She was all wrinkled and curled.
She had leaves in her hair
And twigs on her clothes.

She was flowing down the lake
Like a swan on the river.
She looked so peaceful
But yet so cold,
That was the girl I saw.

You could hear the birds singing
And the water flowing.
The colour of her lips
Were like a blue ink pen.
She had light brown hair
Like bark on a tree.

There was a death in the lake.
A girl I saw.
She was all wrinkled and curled.
She had leaves in her hair
And twigs on her clothes.

Lindsay Herron (13)
Hookergate School

SNOW

I covered a yard
in a silky white blanket,
I covered trees
in big clumps of cream,
I blinded people
with my blizzard,
I killed flowers
with my coldness,
I covered a pond
in a glass pane,
I ate my way
through the trees,
I started falling
to the ground,
I fell without a sound,
I finished off
with a whirl and a wave
and fell down
to my grave,
I fell down sweltering
and lay there melting,
I lay there for good,
never to run again.

Stuart Chapman (13)
Hookergate School

THE LAKE

The lake is a mirror,
A sheet of moonlit glass.
The moon will soon go away,
The lake will never last.

The lake is a mirror,
Silver moonlit glass.
The moon will soon go away,
The lake will never last.

Sarah Hynes (14)
Hookergate School

THE HURRICANE

Hurricanes coming across the land
Wrecking everything on its way
Everybody's running to and fro
Hurry before it's too late.

Trees are tumbling to the ground
While animals are losing their homes
Houses blown up everywhere
Like the land was hit by a bomb.

Children are crying
And the hurricane is near
The bolt of lightning flashed over the land
Lighting up the midnight sky.

The hurricane is here
We are now losing our homes
There's nothing we can do
Because we have nowhere to go.

We drive away in our car
The hurricane has hit our house
There's nothing left to see
We can only scream and shout.

Zoe Snaith (13)
Hookergate School

THE RIVER GRAVEYARD

Chun-Li, the women who I loved for so long,
gasped for air as I strangled her, with vines around her neck.
The night was perfect, her family were there, as well as mine.
The year of our third anniversary; she wished to talk to me alone
she asked, 'So you still love me?'
I replied, 'Yes, do you feel the same way?'
'I don't know any more.'
As my heart sank I felt a bitterness and hatred for myself and for Chun
she could tell she had torn my heart in two.
'I want a divorce,' she replied, 'but can we still be friends?'
She tried to cheer me up.
'After everything I have done for you and the children,
you're after the money. It's always been your concern, hasn't it?'
As I shouted at her a tear came to her eye,
'It looks like it's the only way.'
As she drew her Magnum gun I winded her,
I knew there wasn't any other way.
If she had gotten up she would've shot me,
so I strangled her with the vines then I broke her neck.
As I chucked her in the river all of a sudden my twin came,
'What's going on here?'
I shot him in the head and went back to the party
I posed as 'Uncle' Steve from then, till my dying day.

Robert Hawley (13)
Hookergate School

THE THING ABOUT ME

The thing about me is I don't know what
I don't know why they call me 'swot'

The thing about me is I think I know
Maybe because no one loves me so

The thing about me is I don't know why
Might be because I live in a pigsty

The thing about me is I don't know how
People have to call me a big fat cow.

Cheryl Anderson (11)
Hookergate School

BIRD

Flying high
I'm a bird,
People small on the ground,
Stuck there
They could never fly.

My friends and I fly
High up above,
Our wings spread out
Across the sky,
I dive down to the ground.

I hop around,
I await my breakfast,
The ground is soft
And easy to peck,
The worm is now in my beak.

I'm back in the sky
And night is falling,
Darkness eating up the sky,
I'm going home to my nest,
Goodbye until tomorrow.

Carly Hope (12)
Hookergate School

THE WOMAN

I was walking through the meadows
Watching the sunset
Like a ball of fire taking its last shooting
Flames before it goes out

It was all going great
Then a man approached me
Shouting his head off
I ran but he was too fast
He caught me

I bit him, that only made him worse,
He punched me, I yelled,
He hit again, I thought,
What's going to happen to my kids?
No one knows where I am

He dragged me by my hair
Down the field, he stopped.
It was rather damp and marshy
He picked me up by the scruff of my neck
He threw me into a big lake,
It was full of wood
He put my head under the water

I kicked and kicked
Eventually I lost all of my energy
My breathing stopped
With no one knowing.

Ryan Welsh (13)
Hookergate School

THE GIRL WITH NO PAST OR FUTURE

This girl has no past or future,
No beginning, no end,
All she has is a pale face and pale hands,
Her surroundings are sweet just like lilies.

Flowing along with the current,
Her smooth skin being scratched by the rough reeds,
A rustling of leaves, a scuffling of feet,
She is like water herself.

This girl with no past or future,
She looks so sorry and upset,
She smells so sweet and innocent,
Who could do this to a rose like her?

This girl with no past or future,
How miserable she must have felt,
Flowing down the lake full of spite
She looks so peaceful yet so lonely.

This girl with no past or future
Moving down the lake as fast as a bird,
The sweet smelling makes her so sweet,
She had no beginning and no end.

This girl has no past or future,
No beginning, no end,
All she has is a pale face and pale hands
Her surroundings so sweet just like lilies.

Terri Adamson (13)
Hookergate School

A Lonely Death

He walked me through the forest,
it was damp and cold.
He was shouting and yelling at me
he pushed me, I fell.
My body froze as it hit the cold water.

I'm in a world of my own now,
nobody's there, nobody cares.
What a lonely death.

I'm in my new world, it smells different,
it feels different, it feels cold and damp.
It is different.

Why did he do this?
What did I do?
I guess I'll never know.

Catherine Colesby (13)
Hookergate School

My Golf Poem

I hit the ball straight down the middle
It was as sweet as playing the fiddle
My second shot is in the hole
I just destroyed my opponent's soul
The second hole my drive is in the trees
And I got stung by a lot of bees
The game is now coming to an end
My opponent is going around the bend
Easy win, 5 and 4
My opponent is now crying on the floor.

Christopher Dodd (13)
Hookergate School

The Woman

There was a woman in the pond,
As cold as ice,
Covered in flowers and leaves.
Why am I here?
Who has done this?
All I could hear were the birds singing death.
It was dark,
I was lonely,
Nobody to talk to,
Lying here looking at the birds.
I couldn't move,
It felt like I was suffocating,
I was all cramped up,
I was watching the clouds,
I thought I was in Heaven.
I watched the sun go down
And watched the moon go up,
Then in the morning
I heard the birds singing resurrection.

Anthony McConnell (12)
Hookergate School

The Tiger

There was a big tiger from Asia
that preyed on an African tamer.
One day he laid a trap
when the tiger was having a nap,
tiger awoke and gave it one big stroke
and the tamer was seen never again.

Liam Nichol (11)
Hookergate School

GOODBYE BEACH

Standing at my window,
Looking down to the beach.
A seagull sweeps past me,
Just out of reach.

I see the waves crashing,
So beautiful and blue.
All the creatures of the sea,
Who knows the things they knew.

I see some children playing,
Running across the sand.
With flip-flops on their feet
And ice creams in their hand.

I see the rock pools
And beneath the water I see,
All the crabs and starfish,
Living where they ought to be.

I look up at the sky,
It is such a beautiful day.
The sun is out, the sky is blue,
All the clouds have gone away.

Still standing at my window,
I hear the seagulls screech.
I am going home this afternoon.
Goodbye beach . . .

Beth Atkinson (12)
Hookergate School

DANCE

Dance, don't like it.
Can't do it.
'Ami, come up.'
'No.'
'No?'
'I've got a sore leg.'
'You seemed fine before.'
'I twisted my ankle earlier.'
'Well fine, but it's extra homework for you.'
'What?'
'You heard.'
'Then I think,'
Homework!
I would rather dance in front of millions than extra homework.
'Fine!'
I step up,
Everyone is silent, all staring at me.
Miss turns on the music.
I like this song.
I start to dance.
Hey, it's not as bad as I thought.
I feel the power seep through me.
I wiggle my bum and my hips.
Move my arms and legs.
Everyone's cheering!
All of a sudden,
I am Queen of Dance!

Ami Riddell (11)
Hookergate School

GRANDAD

As I travel to school
having a great day,
going to PE, laughing and smiling,
on my way to maths
with my friends.

On my way to science
then to geography,
having a great day,
finally to history, happy,
the day's nearly over.

Walking down Denton View
on my way to my granny's,
as I walked to the door,
receiving the saddest news ever.

The day my grandad passed away
I was heartbroken,
up until the day we reunite
he will always be in my heart.

I will never forget him,
keeping pictures by my bed,
pictures in my head,
I will never forget him,
the best grandad ever.

Ashleigh Gibson (13)
Hookergate School

THE EARTH

First of all we're up in the clouds,
Where angels dance and sing,
And the mighty God sleeps in his golden lair,
Heaven is what it's called.

Now we're standing on two feet instead of flying,
Standing on the grass surrounded by trees,
Watching the mammals walk by,
The queen and king are ruling us,
Earth's what it's called.

Now we dive into the ocean,
Pacific, Atlantic too,
Fish, whales and dolphins swimming,
No room here for you,
The ocean depths are dark and cold,
You'll not survive the wet.

Now we're digging really fast to reach the centre of the Earth,
We're red and orange lava drips,
The Devil has its home,
Most of us will not go there, but some of us will.

The only place for you and me
Is on the Earth and Heaven,
Where mammals roam and angels dance,
We'll live happy ever after.

Sophie Wardhaugh (11)
Hookergate School

GUESS

There's one,
One of God's creations,
Always sneaking out of sticky situations,
Scratch, scratch, across the floor,
Squeezing through the gaps under the door,
Silently searching for some nourishment
Cringing at the sound of punishment,
This creature lives with you
When it needs an item there is no queue,
Its eyes are dark and beady
Sharp animal instincts are needed,
It has a whip-like tail.
The answer to your question is, no, it's not a whale.
If you still don't know what this animal could be
Go out and look before it's time for tea.

Christopher Kane (13)
Hookergate School

MY HORSE

My horse is black
and I ride on her back,
she has brown eyes
and she's not easy to disguise.

She is a pretty mare
you can't help but stop and stare,
her tail is very long
and she doesn't get things wrong,
her name is Star
and she can run far.

Lucretia Nolan (13)
Hookergate School

THE SUN AND THE MOON

The sun is a marvellous thing,
It sometimes comes out in the spring.
In summer it shines its brightest,
It's hot, steamy and bright,
To some people's delight,
But when night falls,
The sun brightly glows
And sets into the night,
To the moon's delight,
He said goodnight
And out went the sun's bright glow.
When morning came,
The moon went away
And out came the sun again.
The sun said, 'Hello,' and out popped its glow,
That's how the day begins.

Laura Teasdale (13)
Hookergate School

HALLOWE'EN

H allowe'en is a night of fun
A lot of sweets and candy.
L ots of costumes and masks.
L oving the bone-white moon.
O ur mind on sugar.
W e will go trick or treating all night
E ating sweets all night
E ating sweets rots your teeth
N ever sweets again.

Ginna Ord (11)
Hookergate School

FAIRY TALES

Magic tales of mystic places,
Small and large, different faces.
Prince and princess, enchanted castle,
stars and sparkles make their eyes dazzle.

Fairies' wings, gnomes' ears,
Leprechauns' gold, giants' sneers.
Gnomes' hats, pixies' motion,
All make up the perfect potion.

Magic spells from many witches,
Their black cats give children stitches.
Sweetie houses and gingerbread men,
Dwarves getting mixed up again!

Huge giants up in the sky,
Fairies never seem to die.
Tiny people the size of toes,
Do they all exist . . . who knows?

Victoria Johnson (13)
Hookergate School

AS THE DESERT WIND BLOWS

The bright sun warms up the land around,
The light breeze moves the dust on the ground.
No one around, nobody knows
What happens to the sand as the desert wind blows.

The greenish trees on the long, long plain,
The sand smothers the bottoms again and again.
The breeze did this, though nobody knows,
What happens to the sand as the desert wind blows.

You can feel the warmth as sand touches your feet,
The air is dry, there's no one to meet.
Like a dream in your head that nobody knows
Nobody knows what happens as the desert wind blows.

Christopher Wilkinson (13)
Hookergate School

DEAD WOMAN IN A DREADFUL DARK DEAD SEA

A woman is in a pond with her regular clothes,
A flower is in her right hand,
She is floating in water very still, like a statue,
Eyes open, mouth open,
Like a hole in the ground,
Reeds standing like fire burning,
Covering her,
Found at night.
No one knows how she got there,
Not a single fingerprint,
Mark or wound.
Just lying there like she's sleeping,
Flowers around her,
Hay and water,
Silence in the dark
And silence at morning.
Birds singing
And cats screeching.
Total darkness,
The body stands out,
Very creepy
And mysterious.

Vincent Tsang (12)
Hookergate School

SKY-BLUE-PINK

Colours . . .
In the sea and earth and sky
Loads of different colours . . .
Have you ever wondered why?
Why the grass is a luscious green?
Why the sea is blue?
Why the sky is black at night,
Yet red in mornings too?
How come the artists' palette
Is never the same colour twice?
There is spring-green-red and rose-pink-yellow,
And purple-orange is nice . . .
Colours . . .
Red, blue and yellow
Red is mad, yet can be warm
And blue is hard or mellow,
Yellow is the sunshine bright,
There are more colours than you think
Red, green, yellow, blue
But my favourite is sky-blue-pink!

Laura Simmonds (12)
Hookergate School

TOON HEROES

Toon Army, Toon Army
They're really barmy

Nobby Solano is a winger
Shearer's shot is a stinger

Carl Cort is injury-prone
And Ameobi makes me moan

But Bellamy's pace is like lightning
Speed's tackles are really frightening

There is only one real Given
The Toon heroes are now winnin'!

Mark True (13)
Hookergate School

THE GIRL WITHOUT A STORY

Once in the deep, deep marsh
In the deep, deep lake
There was a body
Of a girl without a story.

She had no reason to be floating,
No mark, no cause to be there,
She lay, no past, no future.

The plants and the leaves
Are her eyewitnesses.

No one knows what
Happened to her, because
She's a girl without a story.

She lay there just like the sky,
When the wind is calm.

Why the hell did she
Deserve to die?

No links, no leads,
All but a lifeless girl,
Without a story . . .

Carl Robinson (13)
Hookergate School

DEAD OR ALIVE?

Dead or alive?
We don't really know,
Round the corner
Now let's go.
Her face is white,
Lying on a lake,
For goodness sake.
The weeds are sticking
Up like sticks,
Lying on a bed.
Her a victim
God help this day,
We can't leave her here,
What about her family?

Kim Pattinson (13)
Hookergate School

MY RABBIT

I have a rabbit, Snuffles is his name,
he is black and white,
he has a bit of a brown mane,
he hardly ever bites,
he has fun playing games,
Snuffles is his name.

I have a rabbit, his name is Snuffles,
he has a hutch where he sleeps,
he is so soft when he cuddles,
he looks around the corner to say 'Peep',
that's my best friend Snuffles.

Jill Shepherd (11)
Hookergate School

WHY HER?

A poshly dressed woman
In a pond
Eyes open
Holding a flower
Cold at night
Surrounded by flowers
Wearing a flowery dress.
Being there for hours
Waiting hopelessly for her death.
Silence, that's all
Pale white face
Loneliness
The darkness covers her
And the darkness awaits her.
Her eyes stir into the dark night.

Ashleigh Hetherington (13)
Hookergate School

BABY BLUE EYES

A newborn baby to the house.
All Dad seems to do is shout.
I'll be as quiet as a mouse.
As Baby Blue Eyes crawls about.

Baby Blue Eyes is counting sheep
All I want to do is sleep.
Baby Blue Eyes is getting tall
He's nearly as big as the garden wall.

Baby Blue Eyes is all alone
In his little quiet home.

Sarah Young (13)
Hookergate School

THE EYE

It's here,
It's open to the public,
It winks
And it blinks.

Boats may float through,
It lights up at night,
It crosses the Tyne,
I'm glad it's mine.

It's across the water
And not open to traffic,
So watch you don't trip
And slip.

What is it?

It's the Eye Bridge.

Vicki Manning (13)
Hookergate School

THE SEA

Fierce and feisty, very frightening,
Loud and strong, it hurries along,
Crashing, slapping against the rocks,
Sending out some fearful shocks,
Slicing, slamming, full of might,
Tossing, turning, showing height,
Deep and dark and so controlling,
The sea goes on and the waves keep rolling.

Sam Gardner Little (11)
Hookergate School

BATTLE

Whether a sword, fist or gun
You're in for a shock, it's not fun.
It could be in the sky, sea or land
This present day, guns are at hand.

Battle is bloody, it brings you pain
You cannot stop till the enemy's slain.
Whether in sun, snow, wind or hail
You have one option, that's don't fail.

It could be at school, in the playground
For a good punch up, a reason will be found.
You could be hurt or badly bruised
To stop another fight, measures will be used.

In the past they used swords
It all was funded from rich war lords
The future - who knows what it will hold?
Fought in space, empty and cold.

Daniel Park (13)
Hookergate School

THE TELLY WATCHER

There was a boy who loved to watch telly
But he started to get quite smelly.
He'd stuff his fat face
And couldn't fasten his lace.
He'd rather have a big bowl of jelly.

Craig Wilson (11)
Hookergate School

AN ABORIGINAL SIMILE

There wasn't any stirs among the trees,
No pulse in the earth,
No movement in the void;
The grass was a dry white fire,
Then in the distance rose a cloud,
And a swift rain came,
Like a woman running,
The wind in her hair.

Coming home at the crack of dawn
Waking my father-in-law
With a knock at the door
By my mother-in-law
With a clout and a bunch
And a kick up the bum
So now I know to never wake
My father-in-law!

Scott Murray (11)
Hookergate School

I LOVE HORSES

I love horses, all cuddly and big
Galloping around the field I go
Trot, canter, gallop and more
Giddy up! Giddy up! Come on, let's go!
Mum's waiting at the door, the door.
I love horses, they're my friends.

Jade Hall (12)
Hookergate School

BEST FRIENDS

B est friends giggle,
E very time they meet,
S ing together,
T ogether we will share secrets.

F orever we will keep,
R unning round the football pitch,
I ndividual we are not,
E very time we meet,
N atter we always do,
D ay after day we meet,
S hopping together too.

Laura Brown (11)
Hookergate School

WINTER

As I look onto the ground,
I can hear no summer sound,
Only crunching winter snow,
Everything seems to go slow.

There's an icy feeling in the air,
People still without a care,
Early morning, no one's awake,
I can see a frozen lake,
Then flakes begin to fall,
It will be a white Christmas after all!

Hannah Lefevre (14)
Hookergate School

FEELINGS OF A PERSON

She's cold, freezing, uncomfortable
She's upset, she doesn't care though
She doesn't even know why she's there
All she knows is, she shouldn't be
She shouldn't be in that cold, damp, dark place
She feels upset, angry
Missing her family, her friends
She tries to get up, but she cannot,
She cannot get up
She's trapped, she tries to see clearly
But, in that damp, dark place she's at
She doesn't want to be there
But she is
She's trapped in that cold, dark place
Flowers are around, but she can't smell them
Birds are calling, but she's unaware of them
And that water over her, she can't feel
She doesn't like it
But, even though she can't
She must get up and get out
She tries again
She tries and tries and tries
But, the effort is wasted
She wanted to get out of there
Why am I here?
Why am I here, why?
She asks herself, why?
But it is wasted,
She has been forgotten.

Andrew Dixon (13)
Hookergate School

OPHELIA

Reeds swaying
In the wind
The trees quiver
Right down into water
In the pond
Her body lies
Dressed in flowers
The water dripping
From head to toe
She lies there still
And there is no reply.
How she got there
We don't know.
Was she pushed
Or did she fall?
Gardens so beautiful
Can you see?
Like life and light
In everything
Earth, wind,
Sun and rain,
Most things don't live again.
Her face so cold
And skin so pale
Touches my heart
Then I go the same
In the end.
She lives in the water
Of loneliness.

Sarah Bennett (12)
Hookergate School

A Lady In A Pond

A sunny day,
A lady in a flowery dress,
Lying still in a pond.
Flowers floating around her,
Weeds trying to hide her,
Face
Dark shimmer
In front of her
Her back
The sun shinning its reflection
Flicking
On water.
Everything is still, nothing
Moving.
Is she
Alive?
Dead?
Water lilies lying beside her
Reflecting
On the water
Her hair dangling around her head
Her hair shining with colours
Brown
Blond
Mixed together
Her arms still like statues.

Margaret Bell (12)
Hookergate School

DOLPHINS

Dolphins,
Live in the deep blue sea,
Blue and smooth,
Dolphins.

Dolphins,
Are gentle and soft,
Dolphins are pale to dark blue,
Dolphins.

Dolphins,
Small eyes,
Blow holes on their head,
Dolphins.

Dolphins,
Are smooth,
Dolphins,
Are calm.

I like dolphins,
When I was in America,
The dolphins were cute and cuddly,
They felt soft and smooth,
Dolphins will never hurt you,
So that's why I like dolphins,
Dolphins.

Danielle Lowe (11)
Hookergate School

A Woman Lay

In a stream
Dressed in cream
A woman lay
Covered with flowers

A woman lay in a pond
One hand up
One hand floating
In one hand a water lily was clutched

In a pond
A body lay
Sided by pointed reeds
As the little twigs snapped in half
In the midnight breeze.

The pond woman
Lay so still
With the breaking water the only sound
So soon, so still.

The little flowers
Lying in the water
So still, so lovely
As the breeze strengthened.

The little branches
Snapping and cracking
Swinging over the woman
Like dead fingers.

The lily pads
Stood as still as stones
As the woman's body floated
The woman's face
Was the same as when she died.

Sophie Scott (12)
Hookergate School

AN ICE DEATH

Dead in a pond
Flowers in her hand,
Put to sacrifice.
Left alone,
A tickle of water
Left for the fish.
Cold like ice
Dressed in flowers
Reeds like swords standing straight.
The silence of a graveyard,
Cold as space,
Lifeless body.
As the wind blows no motion,
No light glints from her eye.
As the midnight fog grows,
A lifeless pond.

Stuart Bennett (12)
Hookergate School

THE WATER LADY

The young white lady lying in the pond
With all her life ahead of her
All she can hear is the whistling of the wind
And trickling of the water
All she's thinking of is her family
Deep down they will really miss her
But now her time has passed
And all she's thinking of is her family's future
No one knows who did it or why it happened
Her lips are bright blue and her eyes are wide open,
She looks so miserable
It looks so dark and scary to me
All she can remember is standing at the edge of the water
Singing loudly with the birds,
And then *splash,* she fell straight into the water.
It looks so damp and so cold
But all she can think of is her family and friends.

Nicola Kirby (13)
Hookergate School

THE LYING LADY

The lying lady in the pond wondering why to me.
If only I had one more chance to see my friends and family.
But now that my time has past, I can only hope for happiness
For the future of my kids.
I wonder why that morning in the quiet winter breeze
How I ended up floating down the slippery watery stream.

However I realise that God said it should be,
The last thing I remember is me walking
Down the muddy path singing with the birds
And picking lovely blue, green, pink and orange flowers
And then everything just went blank!

Guy Kelly (14)
Hookergate School

LIONHEART

In the blazing hot sun
Across the African desert,
The king of all kings strolls,
His pack behind him,
With no fear at all.
His mane is beautiful,
Like a golden silk cover
And his eyes,
Bold and strong.

If he catches you . . .
Where he plays and slumbers,
But all the way through the night to
The day he protects.
His young family love him so
But don't understand,
Why he is the king,
Why he is the hero.
Soon they will
Very soon
And they'll love him twice as much!

For he leads the pack to a perfect home.

Ruth McKie (11)
Hookergate School

THE LYING LADY!

The lying lady in the pond
With all her life in front
No one knows how or why
It happened to the lying lady.

Her friends, her husband, no one knows.

The trickling of the water so calm and slow
Who would think to look so hard?
The pond is also dark with weeds and flowers
Overlapping it's also miserable and spooky.

The noises so chilling and smooth
With the trees rustling in the winter breeze
The birds singing so sweet and loud
Who would think to look in a place so far?

Danielle Morland (13)
Hookergate School

WORLD WAR II

Guns are firing, cannons too
This is the start of World War II.

The battlefield is a very grim place
Filled with bodies, blood on their face.

At the hospital, it's a place of healing
But the men inside are seriously bleeding.

Hitler sends his troops forward to attack
The British withstand the charge and the Germans go splat.

The enemy is dying; they're losing their touch
The British can win if they act tough.

D-Day is here and the British front line
Make it over the hill just in time.

Many lives have been lost and soldiers maimed
Let us hope a war like this never happens again.

Steven Banks
Hookergate School

THE WOMAN

Reeds standing as if to hide her.
Weeds on the water as a blanket for her.
Holding a small flower in her hand as if she's lost a loved one.
In a lake, so silent as a church.
Dark like she's in the middle of a forest.
She's cramped in as if she's suffocated.
The sound of the water trickling as if there is a waterfall nearby.
The moonlight as a spotlight on her face.
Flowers blooming near her legs.
Water lilies popping up around her.
Her face as pale as a cloud.
She's young and had everything to live for.
Next to her a path leading from the lake.
The water like crystals but muddy.
Plants around her that look like they have just appeared.
When you look at her the thought of murder comes in.

Lynsey Halliday (12)
Hookergate School

THE SWIMMING GHOST

As she lies in her elegant dress,
Her mouth wide open in shock,
He must have drowned her,
Her must, he must.
As the lilies and daisies
Float beside, they make the
Mood thick and black,
Just like a lonely winter day,
The snow is crisp, the frost is new.
As the shadows of the reeds
Reflect on to her frozen body,
You could almost hear her speak . . .

Jasmine Grey (13)
Hookergate School

HER VOICE

I hear her voice
Every morning and every afternoon
Shouting at the boys,
'Sam, Sam, sit down,'
When she shouts,
My ears scream,
But in silence,
Nobody listens except me,
I watch her turn,
As she puts her head
In her hands,
Poor Mrs Whitside.

Charlotte Graham (12)
Hookergate School

Night Walk

When only a glimpse of light,
Can be seen from the window at night.
The dark people that hide under my bed,
Whisper, so I quickly cover my head.
Under the sheets I hear their breath,
Closer it comes, cold as death.
When I open my eyes, they have gone to hide,
I could not see them, as hard as I tried.
The wind blew harder and then I could see,
The mysterious people looking at me.
Creeping round furniture, not making a sound,
For the owl outside has quietened down,
At last the morning has arrived,
But still I know they've gone to hide.

Victoria Adams (11)
Hookergate School

The Man Who Drank Beer

The man who drank beer,
Ran over a deer,
The deer died so the man cried,
He got out of his truck to see
If there was any luck,
There was none,
So he drove on
And said he would never drink again,
Because the deer had gone through so much pain.

Ashleigh Tiplady (13)
Hookergate School

DARK LASHINGS

The concept of madness,
Or courageous crying,

Good verses bad,
Or bad verses bad,
Confusion, dying and pathetic conflict.

No light, is there,
At the end of a tunnel.
Graphic blindness of blood and inside,
Dirt pricks the face of a hero.

Blast through no man's heart,
Tears of horror, horror of tears,
Offence, defence, madness, valour,
You think not, you feel not,
You know it isn't right.

Unfair carnage, unfair, battle of heartlessness.

Joseph Edward Grugeon-Dixon (13)
Kenton School

INNOCENCE TO HELL

Scatter to scatter, fight to fight,
Gun to gun, within sight.
Throwing death into innocence,
Bursts like a red rose coming out of bud.

Man hides in nature,
Man kills man,
Nature can't prevent hell,
Hell is destroying.

Back home birds are flying,
Dropping their bread,
The wind blows,
Down like a splash it goes.

The British eyes cannot see
What bad is going to be.

Jason Rudowski (13)
Kenton School

CARRY ON, SOLDIER

His chest sticks out and he walks proudly,
That he has been out there killing many,
People say that war is bad,
But to them he says that they are sad.

For they have never had the thrill,
To get to shoot and stab and kill,
To come home victorious with some of your pals
And be a hero with medals.

You're a hero you get praise,
Now all you do is sit and laze,
For you are rich because of this war,
You're going to get more and more.

Although some friends have past on,
But do not worry and carry on,
Because they are up there in a better place,
Looking down with love and grace.

We think of all the death and pain,
But all we say is 'Never again!'

Matthew Dunn (13)
Kenton School

UNTITLED

Bang, crash, smash as the giant birds fly through the sky,
The leaves fall, the planes fall, the suns fall,
The 2nd sun falls into place, the beam of light,
Searching for the target to hit,
It achieves its goal, is this the end? It can't be,
The growl of another plane, heading, coming
Towards us from the coastline,
People panic, terrified, desperate for this revolution to seize.

Bang, crash, smash, one building devastated,
One generation of a family destroyed,
No more, I say no more,
I run into the street holding, sweating,
Hoping that they won't spot me,
I was unfortunate,
I saw the missile-shaped bomb
Heading towards me,
I closed my eyes.

Bang, crash, smash,
Is this the end?
It has got to be!

Robert Carver (13)
Kenton School

IN THE TRENCHES

It was a horrific sight,
The blood splashed,
Our faces went white,
The bombs crashed.
Sirens all around,
To our shock,
We hit the ground,
Like a rock.

It was a horrific sight,
It was clear,
What had happened tonight?
Their faces were full of fear,
The sounds of guns,
Bang, bang, bang, it starts to rain,
People turned around to run,
Then it happened again.

Samantha Shiel (13)
Kenton School

THE LONG-LIVED BOY

There was a man who wanted to get away
From his father straightaway
And he wanted to do it today
As he had wished he went away
And he did it like I say.

He went to the woods and thought he could live there,
But the woodpecker said that he would die
And he said he couldn't live there
Then said, 'Bye-bye.'

He then went to the Copper Castle
Where the princess lived
But he didn't want to die,
So he said, 'Bye-bye.'

He went to the mountain and spoke to the wind,
He said he wouldn't die so he lived there,
He then got bored and wanted to see his dad
So he went home but his dad wasn't there then he said,
'It isn't fair!'

Dean Baxter (13)
Kenton School

THE WAR CURSE

A curse, worse than the Black Death has arrived.
Killing everything in sight.
Choking all but few.
The smoke of death pollutes the air.
Many eyes bled tears,
A plague there has become.

Never get to live your fantasies,
Kill your dreams, relive nightmares,
Laughing skulls smother your sleep,
Devolve your foes, sniper your demons,
Blast your dragons to smithereens.

Fall into hell, die alongside rats,
Hell seems greater than the fear
You've already suffered.
A curse worse than the Black Death conquered all.

James Moore (13)
Kenton School

LIES, LIES, LIES

Above the corn fields
In the blue sky
There comes a whispering bird
There comes horror in everyone's eyes.

Everyone knows where their destiny lies,
They run but there is no truth at the end of all these lies,
The bomb drops and there goes their lives,
How can this be glory, when everyone dies?

The yellow corn fields turn red,
But believe that this isn't the end,
But when would the late sun, rise?
When would this war cease?

Amir Asghari (13)
Kenton School

IN THE TRENCHES - WHY YOU?

It was a horrific sight,
All around, faces were white,
We heard the screams and saw the blood,
This collision was not at all good.

All went silent as they walked around,
Their footsteps were the only sound,
They couldn't stand it, they turned to run,
I cringed as I heard the sound of the gun.

It was a horrific sight,
My face was white,
There he was my good, old bud,
Falling down with a thud.

I screamed with anger,
I never thought,
No sound came out,
I was distraught.

Bye my friend, you had a good life,
I'll be sure to tell your kids and wife,
You fought for your country, they should be proud,
But, why you from the crowd?

Kaylie Mulholland (13)
Kenton School

ON THE BATTLEFIELD

The air was dusty,
The sky pitch-black,
The smell of blood,
The flying flack.

The noise of gunshots,
The sound of planes,
The sight of dead men,
The blood washed away as it rains.

This is the war that lasted forever,
This is the war that people said would never end,
But as they say, never say never.

Kayleigh Balmer (13)
Kenton School

THE WALL

Noble and honourable they go to war,
When they go through that door,
Beyond that wall that blinds us all,
In the line of fire they will fall.

One man ends another man's life,
Not thinking of that man's wife,
He does not care if he goes to Hell,
Because in his eyes he's already there.

Matthew Lee (13)
Kenton School

GWNETH

She is a butterfly,
A coat as rich as mahogany,
As pretty as a flower,
As light as an angel,
I love being near her.

We do everything together,
We share lollies and drinks
And go on picnics together,
She fills my life with love,
I love her to bits.

I would cry without her,
She is my best friend,
My second pony Gwneth.

Deile Turnbull (14)
Ponteland County High School

MY MOST PRECIOUS POSSESSION

It is the keeper of history,
In the most unlikely of places,
As round as the setting sun,
Sophisticated and accurate as the owl,
Grey and smart,
Hiding until I request its presence,
Glad when I get the desired answer,
As it is my watch.

Adam Soulsby (14)
Ponteland County High School

STAIRWAY TO HEAVEN

He was my best friend,
He was strong and brave,
Standing tall and mighty,
He was my best friend,
And so,
I walked that last walk with him,
Straight as a die, bold as brass,
He walked that last walk with me,
Holding our past like a play,
Never to be re-enacted.

He was my gallant hero,
That last walk drew my tears,
I wish I could have stopped that last walk,
Up the hill,
But no man could stop my best friend,
My pony going up his
Stairway to Heaven.

Nikki Gilbertson (14)
Ponteland County High School

THE LOCKET

It is a dream,
Timeless and unchanging,
Capturing eternity,
A precious memory,
Sealing time,
Gold,
My view of something past,
A locket.

Sarah Duggan (14)
Ponteland County High School

LORD OF THE RINGS

Lord of the rings
(Otherwise known as:
Lord of the competition entries).

It is glass.

Smooth,
Seamlessly continuing.

Glowing gold,
Controlling my thoughts,
My memories,

Of the day it was given

My ring.

Kate Wallis (14)
Ponteland County High School

THE KEEPER

It is the night's sky,
Full of many things, the stars and the moon,
Somehow this small, tough keeper of stars
Came into my possession.
How this wonderful, amazing object
Came into this world,
Nobody knows!
The object of my affection,
Is not the keeper of stars,
But my small, black wallet,
The keeper of money, credit cards
And all things personal.

James Fisher (15)
Ponteland County High School

HARRODS

It is a dove,
As soft as fur,
As clean as water,
As cute as a puppy,
Cuddly,
Quiet,
Timid,
It has been with me all my life,
It is 'Harrods' my teddy bear.

Jay Mihcioglu (14)
Ponteland County High School

MOB

It is as light as a pen,
It is as compact as a car on a camping trip,
It is as ripe as a tomato,
It is as blue as the sea,
It is as revolutionary as a PC,
It is a mobile.

Adam Houghton (14)
Ponteland County High School

MY DIAMOND

The dazzling diamond,
Her sparkling dress,
Her bright, ice-blue eyes,
Her contrasting plain white socks.

Funny and loud
Stands out in a crowd
My sister
Who makes me so proud.

Danielle Blacklock (14)
Ponteland County High School

THE GOLDEN TROPHY

I ran like a cheetah to get this,
It's as gold as a carrot,
It's marble resembles a fireplace,
It's as if somebody won this,
I can't believe a boy could run
And be so brutal to get the trophy.

David Collis (14)
Ponteland County High School

IT'S AS VALUABLE AS GOLD TO ME

As white as chalk,
As black as night,
As stripy as a zebra,
It gives me enthusiasm,
It makes me happy,
I love to wear it,
It makes me loyal,
I love to watch them . . .
Let us see them win!

Garry Wilson (14)
Ponteland County High School

It's My Car

It's as yellow as a bee,
As it speeds down the long windy roads,
As it stops to refuel,
It glugs down forty quid or more,
It gives a loud roar and we're at home,
Can't wait to drive my Aston Martin.

Andrew Hayes (14)
Ponteland County High School

The Mighty Nick Sword

It's as sharp as a bee sting
And as quick as an eye.

As dark as the shadows,
But shines like the sun.

It cuts through anything,
Because that's my mighty Nick sword.

Nicholas Mathieson (14)
Ponteland County High School

Untitled

Once as shiny as tinfoil,
The silver glows like the sun
And glimmers like polished leather,
The structure is like chains
And as strong as steel,
An old silver chain.

Ryan Johnson (14)
Ponteland County High School

GOOD LUCK CHARM

The claw of an eagle,
Gripped tight around a crystal ball,
Past memories attached to a charm,
The charm is the future,
Go ahead with a smile,
Purple like the mysteries asked,
The silver like a child.

Amy Daley (14)
Ponteland County High School

THE WORDS THAT MEAN SO MUCH

It is the sun
On a blue background it stands
So sweet to hear those words
Computer typed
It looks so good
My grandparents
Their words call out loudly.

Sam Taylor (14)
Ponteland County High School

FLUFF BALL

It is brown fluff,
Cute, little, playful, chubby, cuddly,
It is labelled with a tag,
Adorable, quiet, lovely, lively, fast,
It can beg with its eyes,
Dashing, panting, begging, whining, barking,
It . . . is a dog.

Adam McEnaney (14)
Ponteland County High School

BLACK AND WHITE

It's the lion's roar,
Powerful, loud, melodic, strong and deep,
Years of my life spent pounding the keys,
Showing the colours of the Tyne,
My stress relief,
My keyboard.

John Thomson (14)
Ponteland County High School

ROTTEN FRIDGE

It is colder than ice,
Square as a circle,
As smooth as a walrus,
It opens to the smell of must,
All I see is cabbage and dust,
Then behind a can of Spam,
Behold, I find a packet of ham.

Michael Carr (14)
Ponteland County High School

DADDY'S RING

Looking up at me like a distant memory,
A band to signify eternity,
A love that was broken prematurely,
Given to me in loving memory,
It will stay in my heart as a piece of history,
Daddy's little girl never got a chance.

Holly Lillico (14)
Ponteland County High School

STRUMMING FOR FUN

Sounding loud as a jet plane,
As black as the night,
I love to play those strings,
A song that makes me happy,
Playing slow, fast, heavy, light,
Whatever I feel like,
My electric guitar.

Alex Sandercock (14)
Ponteland County High School

SILVER HEART

It is a star,
It is a heart,
Silver, shining, gleaming,
Glittering, glistening,
Reminds me of a happy day,
A necklace.

Sarah Duffy (14)
Ponteland County High School

BETSY

It is a cloud,
It is as old as me,
Its eyes are black,
Its fur was white,
Now grey,
Lasting longer than my life,
My rabbit teddy.

Alison Holmes (14)
Ponteland County High School

JOSH

He was my life, he stood
Strong,
Proud,
Sometimes happy,
Sometimes sad,
He cheered up when times were bad,
I think of him every day
And in my heart he lives,
Until this day,
I haven't forgot,
Josh,
My dog.

Danielle Hawkins (14)
Ponteland County High School

A GHOST

It is a ghost,
Big ears,
Apples as pants,
He's sad because he died as a small boy,
But he's got a bushy tail
And suns as hands,
A very strange ghost,
He doesn't know what he is.

Lindsey Willis (14)
Ponteland County High School

MY DOG THAT TRAGICALLY DIED

My dog Tosca all grey and old,
Who always warmed me when I was cold,
He used to eat and sleep all the time,
Never bad enough to commit a crime.

But then one day he ran out the door,
Never to return,
I wish I could see that dog again,
He's still a memory in my brain.

One afternoon the news came through,
My dog had been ran over,
I ran as fast as I could, out onto the lawn,
I sat out there by myself and had a great big mourn.

I still love my dog named Tosca,
I will never forget him.

Craig Hodgson (11)
Usworth Comprehensive School

GIRLS

The problem with girls is they're just so picky,
They actually think that they are quite pretty,
They dress up in skirts and flowers in their hair,
What they don't know is bugs will be there,
They walk down the street and also skip,
The perfume they wear keeps making me sick!

David Smith (12)
Usworth Comprehensive School

SCHOOL RULES

This is an important matter
How we should behave at school
We should get along much better
When we can obey the rules.
Don't run down the corridors,
We're learning!
Never bully,
Never punch,
Watch your manners, eat your lunch,
We're learning!
This is an important matter
How we should behave at school
We should get along much better
When we can obey the rules.

Lee Atkinson (11)
Usworth Comprehensive School

DOGS

Dogs are playful,
Dogs are faithful.

They come in different shapes and sizes
And different types and breeds.

Dogs are playful,
Dogs are faithful.

They're so cute and cuddly.

Dogs are playful,
Dogs are faithful.

Jemma Burton (11)
Usworth Comprehensive School

MORNING

The sun shines through my window,
The birds tweet as they play their morning song,
The trees sway from side to side,
The wind huffs and howls,
It all happens as I wake up.

The flowers bloom from the morning wind,
The grass seems greener than ever before,
The angels look down from open Heavens,
A new day, a new start,
It all happens as I wake up.

All from yesterday, becomes past,
All from today, becomes present,
All my sadness turns into joy,
All my moods turn into joy,
It all happens as I wake up.

Sophie Minnis (12)
Usworth Comprehensive School

HALLOWE'EN

Black cats go prowling through the night,
Poor passers-by receiving a fright,
Then there are dragons, fire-breathing beasts,
Eating people is their favourite feast.

Witches on brooms flying so high,
Scattering the clouds as they fly,
Spirits swooping all around,
Very quiet not making a sound.

Chelsey Taylor (12)
Usworth Comprehensive School

NOBODY KNOWS ABOUT MY BULLIES

My mam says I'm a jewel, but I'm treated
Like a mule at school, the bullies think it's
Cool to throw a stool or duck me in the pool,
Though it's against school rules, but it's like
They're fed on fuel, even at dinner,
They take the good stuff and I'm left with gruel.

Break time. They stash my cash, as they bash my head,
Mash my face and lash my legs.
I've a rash where they've dumped their ash from their ciggies,
I might as well wear a geek sash.

The pain, it feels insane as it pumped through my veins,
I'm feeling lame though I always get the blame.
It feels like I've been hit with a cane by the bullies
Who are inhumane and which must never be named.
It's always the same plain, me I'm always their target
I'm always their aim.

Kayleigh Abbott (13)
Usworth Comprehensive School

WHEN THE WEATHER CHANGES

A touch of cold on an autumn night,
A touch of rain on a summer day,
When the weather changes hot to cold,
Wrap up tight and don't be cold.
A touch of sun on a winter day,
A touch of snow on a springtime day,
When the weather changes from cold to hot,
Put your sunglasses on and enjoy the sun.

Christopher James French (11)
Usworth Comprehensive School

MY SANCTUARY

In day it is white,
At night it is black,
When I flick a switch, it's pink.

Candles everywhere,
Incense sticks burning,
With a scent that lasts for days.

A CD plays on,
The voice comes to life,
Soothing all stress that's kept in.

Oriental art,
Inspiring visions,
Leaves the feeling of relief.

My sanctuary,
A long life Eden,
I know will always save me.

Louise Donkin (12)
Usworth Comprehensive School

SPOOKY POEM

S   hivering coldly down my spine,
P   rickling pins and needles hiding from what lies within,
O   wls marching in the attic, scratching along.
O   nly now I freeze and shiver with horror over what I see,
K   illers running wild, running after your little child,
Y   our horror is ruling your life,

    So beware you're in for a scare . . .

Claire Reid (13)
Usworth Comprehensive School

I LOVE DOLPHINS

I love dolphins,
I love them so much,
I love the way they play with people
And I love their special touch.

I love dolphins,
I'd love to swim with them,
I love the way they swim freely
And I love the little baynes.

I love dolphins
One day my dream will come true,
Just to swim with dolphins,
Is what I'd love to do.

Nicola Bain (12)
Usworth Comprehensive School

SPOOKY STORY

Hooting of the owl
People at the fire camp
The cackle of the fire
Rummaging in the bushes,
Listen, *bang, bang, bang,*
What is that?
Hoot, hoot,
Help, help, help,
Everything is quiet,
Hoot, hoot, hoot,
Goes the owl in the dark of night.

Carley Lawrence (13)
Usworth Comprehensive School

HELL!

Fireballs flying,
Rushing through the sky!

In the middle of the earth,
You'd wish you would die!

But that's impossible,
When you're already dead!

People walking about,
Without their head!

The last thing I heard,
Was the ringing of a bell!

By now you should know
That I'm in Hell!

Chris Davies (11)
Usworth Comprehensive School

GREEN IS . . .

Green is the colour of the grass,
Green is as green as a flower,
Green is as green as a tree,
Green is as green as a greenfly,
Green is as green as a grape,
Green is as green as a frog,
Green is as green as an apple,
Green is as green as a lizard,
Green is green!

Zoe Bell (11)
Usworth Comprehensive School

THE SECRET AT THE BOTTOM OF MY GARDEN

I tiptoe outside in my bare feet
And run out on the icing-white grass
For I am here just go greet,
The secret at the bottom of my garden.

The wildflower bush peers over my face,
All behind is my footprint trace
The secret place is in one pace,
Yes the secret at the bottom of my garden.

The sun is rising, I'm nearly there,
My secret takes a lot of loving care,
My secret at the bottom of my garden.

I kneel down in my nighty gown
And suddenly appears a frown,
I tiptoe back into my bed,
For the secret at the bottom of my garden is . . .
Dead!

Laura Handy (11)
Usworth Comprehensive School

CHRISTMAS

The kids run down the stairs,
Some still holding their teddy bears,
They see the presents and they don't even stop to stare,
They rip the wrappers open like they just don't care
And in the air, you can hear the tear, tear, tear.

Sean Herron (11)
Usworth Comprehensive School

HALLOWE'EN

Silence in the dark street . . .
Knock, knock, knock,
Witches at the doorstep
Vampires too!

Ugly faces saying trick or treat,
Walking around in the street,
Dressing up is cool on Hallowe'en day,
Put all the effort in, hope I get a pay.

Pumpkins glowing in the dark,
Taking a short cut through the park,
Taking my sister round the streets,
Getting lots of yummy sweets!

Cheryl Robinson (11)
Usworth Comprehensive School

HALLOWE'EN

Hallowe'en is for people to enjoy,
Hallowe'en is for little girls and boys,
Hallowe'en is a spooky time,
Hallowe'en is pumpkins full of slime,
Hallowe'en is witches on broomsticks,
Hallowe'en is scarecrows made of sticks,
Hallowe'en is werewolves howling,
Hallowe'en is ghosts and spirits frowning,
Hallowe'en is for children to trick or treat,
Hallowe'en is for parents to eat.

Ashleigh Ord (11)
Usworth Comprehensive School

HALLOWE'EN

Creeping and crawling
All night long
In the night
I heard a song
The cockerel crows
Morning has come
Night has gone.

Children come out
Hip hip hooray
It's Hallowe'en
All day.
Then six o'clock
Comes, kids go
Trick or treating,
Come back at seven,
But they're already away.

Alexandra Muter (11)
Usworth Comprehensive School

DREAM DAY

Fall, leaves, fall; die flowers away;
Lengthening night and opening day;
Every leaf speaks different to me,
Fluttering from the autumn tree.
I shall smile then sing when weather snows;
Blossom is when the rose should grow;
I shall jump and shout when night falls.

Then the night will go.

Ryan Ellis (12)
Usworth Comprehensive School

THE PUPPY DOG

This puppy dog is cuddly and soft,
When it is night-time he sleeps in the loft.
When he is sleeping, he looks so cute
And when he is like this, he is so like a mute.

When morning comes, he is really hyper,
After breakfast he acts like a fighter,
He is only like this on the park,
Where he runs and begins to bark.

When he gets home he starts to play,
Even though he has been out all day,
He starts to get tired and lies on his bed
And dreams happily for the day ahead.

Lindsay Purvis (13)
Usworth Comprehensive School

MONKEY POEM

Monkeys are full of fun and laughter,
What can you do after?
Play with sand or work and stand.

They eat bananas all day long,
While they sing a little song like ooh ah ooh.

They swing from tree to tree and never hurt
Their wonky knees,
Some are fat and don't like cats,
That's what monkeys are like.

Laura Rackstraw (11)
Usworth Comprehensive School

CHRISTMAS

C hristmas is a time when families get together,
H appy times at Christmas,
R eindeer galloping through the sky,
I n from the cold on Christmas Day,
S anta asleep in his rocking chair,
T ime for us to come in from playing,
M ams and Dads tired,
A t 12.00 clock time for bed,
S leepyhead go to bed.

Stephanie Johnson (11)
Usworth Comprehensive School

CHRISTMAS

C hristmas is a happy time,
H anging holly on the door,
R iding on your sledge in the snow,
I cicles hanging from the rooftops,
S tockings hanging from the wall,
T he joys to play with so much fun,
M isletoe could mean a kiss,
A ll excited couldn't wait,
S anta's been it's so great.

Charlotte Walton (11)
Usworth Comprehensive School

MY GRANDAD

My grandad is alive in my mind
I miss my grandad
He always had time for me,
He told me stories on his knee.

He took me out to the park
He always made me laugh
With a dog called Tig
Who fetched him a twig.

Gemma Horn (11)
Usworth Comprehensive School

GRANDAD

It's not that long ago that
My grandad passed away.
My life just does not seem the same,
I think about him every day,
Whilst I dream the night away,
But now that he has gone,
I have to learn to go on,
I know his soul will carry on,
I know he will wait for me
Until it's my turn to join him.

Ashleigh Lupton (13)
Usworth Comprehensive School

MIDNIGHT FRIGHT

S hivering and squealing in my bed,
P raying for the sun to rise,
O h the worst is not over, it's midnight now,
O h there's that noise, oh help me please,
K illers and thrillers bang on the door,
Y es it's morning, phew that was scary.

Lee Ridley (14)
Usworth Comprehensive School

TODAY I FEEL COLOUR

Today I'm feeling red,
My blood is curdling, my brain is boiling,
I'm afraid someone may end up dead!
My fists are ready to punch the air,
I don't even care,
Tomorrow I may feel yellow.

Today I feel yellow,
Yellow is calm and mellow,
I feel yellow on a warm spring day,
I could lay in the grass all May,
Tomorrow I may feel blue.

Today I feel blue,
Blue is sad and depressed,
I hope you don't feel like this too,
All I want to do is cry,
Hopefully, this feeling will pass by,
Tomorrow I may feel green.

Today I feel green,
Green is sick, queasy and obscene.
The toilet is calling you,
You just know you are going to spew.
Tomorrow I might just sleep,
To end my rather colourful week.

Danny Needham (11)
Usworth Comprehensive School

HALLOWE'EN

Hallowe'en is a scary night
When all of the adults turn off the lights
Where little kids go to trick or treat
Then their parents nick all the sweets.

Hallowe'en is a night of fright
It is also a silent night
When the witches go for a flight
Hallowe'en is a scary night.

Sarah Rossiter (11)
Usworth Comprehensive School

WHO OR WHAT IS SHE?

Rei, the name means nothing,
She isn't even a human being,
Why is she here?
What is she?

She is obsolete, nothing,
Nothing more than a mere clone,
She pilots a robot prototype,
It is accident prone.

Her life, she has nothing else,
She is very strong,
In her heart,
She just lives, forever long.

Why is she here?
She has no objectives,
No lifelong dreams,
Even in life-threatening situations,
I hear no screams.

What is she?
As before a clone,
Plus the mere flesh and bone,
Has she no real home?

Mark King (14)
Usworth Comprehensive School

SCHOOL

When the bells go, school starts
first it's maths, we play darts
not every lesson is such fun
some make me want to run

After break we've got tech
often a pain in the neck
the time doesn't seem that fast
this lesson seems to last

After tech it's lunch
when we have a Munch Bunch
after lunch it's geog
we take it in, no, maybe not

Then the bore of the day
history, what can I say?
We go home at the end of the day
but it's not the end, we have to play.

Nick Shotton (13)
Usworth Comprehensive School

SPOOKY POEM

H orrified I would not move,
O ut there was someone waiting for us,
R ound the corner waiting for us,
R evenge he wanted on us, we went
O ut and he was gone, he disappeared so I
R an for my life.

Vicky Mason (13)
Usworth Comprehensive School

Why, Why, Why, All The Time!

'Why? Why? Why?' said the man of old age
He was sick of his life
People always giving him a good old stabbing
In the back with a knife
His life was a terrible pity
Like a raggy old dog wandering the city
He had no friends
He had no wife
She had run away with his treasured delight
Held tight, escaping in the night
No one would help him
He had no job
Because they all regarded him as a slob
'Why, why, why?' he would cry. 'If only I had never left my home
I could sit by the fire and eat till I die
Why? Why? Why?' said the man.
'This is how I want it, all lonely and cold
But most of all unwanted.'

Harry Robson (14)
Usworth Comprehensive School

Autumn Days

Red, crispy leaves,
Falling and falling,
Falling off the orange trees,
At autumn night,
I got a fright,
It was Hallowe'en.

Dean King (11)
Usworth Comprehensive School

SPOOKY POEM

Something slithering in the night.
As the wind pounds still on sight.
The shadows are scary as they pass.
The door knocks when not locked.
Wolves' yelps coming from the forest.

Brent Johnson (13)
Usworth Comprehensive School

DOOMED

D ark nights are here with ghouls and monsters,
O r many people dying,
O f fright and pain,
M urders roaming the streets,
E verybody running,
D amaging everything in their sight.

Happy nightmare, ha, ha, ha.

Dee Robson (13)
Usworth Comprehensive School

DARKNESS

Raining heavily and howling winds,
There it began, the clashing windows.
Walking down the dark spooky alley looking around,
All I could see was rats and bats,
The yowl of a cat and the howl of a dog,
I began to run.

Karl Horn (13)
Usworth Comprehensive School

MY CAT, DELILAH

She's my cat and she's the best,
If she was lost, I'd never rest,
Her name is Delilah, it's written in gold,
She obeys me, her owner and does as she's told.

Oh sweet, sweet Delilah, your smile
Lights up my heart,
Oh sweet, sweet Delilah, I wish we
Weren't apart,
But that was the past and now you are gone,
But in my mind your presence goes on.

You'll stay in my memory for all eternity,
I think of you as if you're still sitting on my knee.

Emma Naisby (11)
Usworth Comprehensive School

MY MAM

I hate my mam to bits,
Cause she ran away with her boyfriend Pete.
I'm happy now she's gone,
But hate her for what she's done.

I'm very happy with my dad,
Because she's treated me so bad,
I love my dad so much and he loves me.
My mam didn't even say goodbye,
So I cried and I cried until
I could cry no more.

Samantha Wallace (13)
Usworth Comprehensive School

HALLOWE'EN

Hallowe'en is for children to enjoy,
Hallowe'en is for girls and boys.

Hallowe'en is for children to trick or treat,
Hallowe'en is for children to eat their sweets.

Hallowe'en is costumes and scary masks,
Hallowe'en is having a blast.

Hallowe'en is vampire bats,
Hallowe'en is witches with black cats.

Sophie Parish (11)
Usworth Comprehensive School

I LIKE YOU

I like you,
I like you,
I really must say I must
Because you're the only
Person that I can really trust!

Mark Tulip (13)
Usworth Comprehensive School

JOLLY HOLIDAYS

Holidays are always fun,
Sunbathing all day in the blazing sun,
Night-time comes and you meet a fella,
Good-looking and even a truth-tella.

Boogying away on the dance floor,
When morning came my feet were sore,
We strolled the beaches all day long,
Not one minute of it felt wrong.

Joanne Meikle (13)
Usworth Comprehensive School

MY MATES

My friend Stacey is a better lass with
A lot of class, but you just can't get anyone better.

I've got another friend Hannah,
You just can't explain, she's more crazy than me.

And then there's little Laura,
She's rock-solid, she's got this strategy when
She fights, she's like a little rocket,
When she comes out the door,
She's saying, 'Come on give me more.'

Rebecca Rowntree (13)
Usworth Comprehensive School

MARCUS

M is for massive, mad and moody,
A is for anxious, angry and alert.
R is for rude, red and ragged,
C is for calm, cool and cautious.
U is for unhappy, ugly and upset,
S is for smiling, smelly and snoopy.

Marcus Javan (12)
Whitburn School

BONFIRE NIGHT

Whizzing, fizzing and a whoosh of light,
All come together on Bonfire Night.
Hiss, sizzle, and a bang and boom,
Guy Fawkes' day is coming soon.

5th November, Bonfire Night,
Fireworks shooting into the night.
Children cheering, sparklers burning,
Bangers cracking, Catherine wheels turning.

Potatoes baking, hot dogs sizzling,
Watch the fireworks, zooming, whizzing.
The bonfire crackling, burning bright,
November the 5th is my favourite night!

Laura Kirk (13)
Whitburn School

KYE

Kye's time with us has come and gone,
It was time for him to go.
He led such a quick and humble life,
But was loved by many so.
Oh how I wish he could be here,
Watching me write this poem.
He was the cutest dog alive,
I am sure the nicest known.
In loving memory of him,
I, John Romans, write this poem.

John Romans (12)
Whitburn School

FIRE

Fire, fire on the stair,
Fire, fire, everywhere.
Fire is now getting in the house,
I will scatter, like a mouse.

Everywhere there are fires,
Melting all coatings of the wires.
Over the fence the fire is going,
All of the time growing and growing.

Through the garden, muddy and soggy,
Up in the sky it is getting foggy.
Along comes the fog all wet and damp,
Time to put out that fiery lamp.

Jonathon Phinn (11)
Whitburn School

SWEET SURRENDER

He hung around the churchyard, deep into the night,
He looked around, impatient, waiting for souls to blight.
Cracking his knuckles and grinning so mad,
Ready to pounce on them, take all that they had.
He came from round the corner as I passed a tomb
And I knew then he would send me to my doom.
Laughing as I panicked over my blunder,
He then struck a blow that tore my soul asunder.
As the dizzying blow forced my brain to render,
I felt the pain wash over me and succumbed to sweet surrender.

Matthew Ball (14)
Whitburn School

ON THAT SPECIAL DAY

In the dark of the night,
In the light of the day,
Many of us pray
For that special day

When the world will change
To fulfil our hearts
With joy and peace,
No end, just a start!

Starvation will stop,
Terrorism will stop,
Any form of abuse will stop

On that day,
That special day,
When the day is not only light,
But also the night!

Mellisa Sanders (13)
Whitburn School

CHRISTMAS

C hristmas is just around the bend,
H oles in stockings Mum needs to mend.
R udolph's nose is glowing red,
I magining presents in my head,
S now is slowly falling down,
T ime to shop in the town.
M usic playing right into the night,
A ngels and candles burning bright.
S anta's coming, hip hip hooray, I can't wait for the very next day!

Lucy Walker (12)
Whitburn School

THE WEATHER

I am the weather,
I am the supremacy,
I can be the bane of men
Or I can bring them ecstasy.

Nobody knows what form I'll take,
A thunderstorm, or a drought, maybe
I could shrivel anyone to a cinder,
A giant, or just a tiny baby.

I could squeeze the life from this planet
Like water from a sponge.
I could mask the rays of the sun
And the Earth into darkness plunge.

I am more effective
Than any barricade you'll ever see.
You may try to read my mind,
But alone, you won't succeed.

Emma Naughton (12)
Whitburn School

THE DODGY POEM

Bing, bong, bash,
The water went splash.
'Smack, crack, whack,'
Said good old Jack.
'Fizz, biz, wiz,'
Said little baby Liz.
'Why are you crying?'
Said big, old Ryan.
'Because the poem has ended.'

Ryan Dent (12)
Whitburn School

ME

This is *me:*

I'm as fast as a cheetah,
I'm a world-beater.

I'm as greedy as a gannet,
Stop eating - I cannot.

I'm as brainy as a chimp,
But I am no wimp.

I'm as strong as a bear,
Even though I don't care.

I'm as smelly as an ox,
No one goes near *my* socks!

I'm as thin as a shrimp,
(Or so people think.)

I'm as busy as a bee,
But I'm proud to be *me!*

Jonathan Dixon (11)
Whitburn School

WAR

War is terrible.
It is filled with hatred and blood.
The only thing to save people
Is hospitality from the good.

When you're young
You think it's a game,
But it suddenly hits you,
It's not and it might know your name.

When war breaks out,
World leaders shout
And try to help and be good-hearted,
But this shouldn't happen,
Because war shouldn't
Break out.

Gavin Graham (12)
Whitburn School

IT

It affects people all around the world,
And yes it can be cured,
But if you're so busy fighting these things,
The blood may not be going to the limbs.

The legs and arms may have to be amputated
And replaced with ones which are imitated.
He is no different, he's stayed the same,
But people may stare and what a shame.

You will look, then glance, then stare,
And wonder why his arms and legs are not there.
This could send him round the bend
And stop you and him from making friends.

If you see him in the street, it would be good to say, 'Hi,'
He's not that different from you or I.
It affects people all around the world
And yes, meningitis can be cured.

But if you see him in the street,
Just to show you care,
When he passes you by,
Smile and do not stare.

Imogen Nicholson (12)
Whitburn School

SEPTEMBER 11TH

September 11th is a day we all recall
For many it was the saddest day of all,
So many lives were needlessly lost,
So many families left counting the cost.

But out of the tragedy there came hope,
Mankind was determined that we would all cope.
So many people were helpful and brave,
Risking themselves if a life could be saved.

A year later we still can't believe the madness,
We are left with memories and a lingering sadness,
But we won't let our lives be consumed by sorrow,
We must all work together to build a better tomorrow.

Emma Landsbury (13)
Whitburn School

THE EARTH

The Earth is a place where people can't get along,
But it is the only place where I can belong.
The Earth is changing at a rapid pace,
I don't believe I can keep up with this race.
There isn't time to stop and wait
As we all have the same fate.
Death is life
So why do we strive
To be more
Than the person before?
I am the best that I can be,
Even though people do better than me.

Liam Bruce (14)
Whitburn School

SPOOKY HOUSE

Everything spooky in the house,
All you hear is a squeak of a mouse
And I need to get out!

Everything spooky in the midnight house,
I feel like I am squeaking like a louse
And all the cats are
Scratching at the door.

If they don't stop it,
I will scream myself
Out!

Everything spooky in the house,
All the mice are freaking me out.
I need to leave this house
Or I will scream the creepy mice
Out!

Stacey Banks (12)
Whitburn School

SNOW

Morning rising all around,
What has the evening chill left on the ground?
A thick carpet of pure white snow,
Deadens the sound as people come and go.
Children are laughing and playing in the street,
Making incredible patterns in the snow with their feet.
I must get dressed and quickly go,
To leave my own message
In the newly fallen snow.

Amy Edmondson (12)
Whitburn School

THE RAINFOREST

Chop, chop, chop
Goes the rainforest of Brazil.
'Timber!' yells the culprit.

The panda sits in his tree,
Then he casts those big black eyes at me,
It makes me think
That tomorrow, he could be no more.

Another orang-utan gone for the population,
Another panda,
Another sloth,
Another snake

And as the numbers go down,
Just a few people begin to frown,
As global warming increases.

As the ozone layer thickens,
People take no notice,
But I know the world is dying.
Slowly . . . slowly . . . slowly.

Laura Stephenson (14)
Whitburn School

ME, MYSELF AND I

Me, myself and I
Are as fast as a fly,
So we won't die.

Me, myself and I,
Are as loud as a horn
When I yawn.

Me, myself and I
Are as clever as a fish
Because I live in a dish.

Me, myself and I
Are as strong as a rock,
Not as a block.

Peter Collinson (11)
Whitburn School

STOP! THINK! REMEMBER!

Remember September 11th 2001,
How it all happened one year ago.
One minute the Twin Towers there,
Sparkling smartly in the sapphire sky,
The next, lying still on the deep,
Dark, death-taking ground.
How it all happened, so fast and so soon,
They came without warning,
Like two bolts of fire from the hand of evil.
What became of those terrorist people?
What about the children in the planes
Knowing they weren't going to survive?
Telling their parents that they were going to die,
And the parents hearing their children's voices
For the final and hindmost time.
Imagine how it would feel to know that you
Weren't going to see your family and friends forever,
You can only hear their voices for the last time.
What do you think of those terrorists?
Stop! Think! Remember!

Tonya Robson (12)
Whitburn School

FEAR

I hate fear,
But fear is what drives me.
Fear could be a fear of heights or spiders,
But fear is what drives me.

Fear keeps driving me to overcome something,
Fear is what keeps me alive,
But this could also kill me,
Fear is what drives me.

Fear stops me doing things that come to harm me,
But fear also pushes me to do things that could harm me.
This is what pushes me,
But fear is what drives me.

I have become one with fear,
I live with fear
And fear lives with me.
It guards and pushes me to do things.
I like *fear!*

Christopher Lester (13)
Whitburn School

SCHOOL

Every day you wake up for it,
It's as deep as a pit.
The teachers are not nice,
It's a chance like 1 to 6 on a dice.

Your pen runs out of ink,
It's a trip to the head's sink.
Don't talk in the school,
It's against the rule.

It's the devils day and night,
The pants you wear are too tight.
Don't be such a fool,
Yea, school is really quite cool.

Gavin Haswell (11)
Whitburn School

BUTTERFLY KISSES

I can see a red rose in the garden,
I can see an aeroplane flying,
I can see a green car passing,
I can see a dancing bear,
Butterfly kisses everywhere.

I can do anything I want,
I can do a cartwheel,
I can do whatever I want,
I can blow kisses in the air,
Butterfly kisses everywhere.

I can walk a mile,
I can make my bed,
I can love my family,
I can be helpful and share,
Butterfly kisses everywhere.

I can be nice to my friends,
I can help others.
I can do things that I know are right,
But I always remember any time, anywhere,
Butterfly kisses are in the air.

Natasha Curry (12)
Whitburn School

HOMEWORK

Homework is the Devil's toy,
Drains freedom from a boy.

Burn, burn, burn, homework.
Get rid of it
Or die.

Way, way, way down in evil Hell
The Devil is writing today's homework,
So you will have no freedom after the bell.

Run, run, run, homework,
It's after you,
You'll die.

Doing homework is like getting murdered,
Don't let its cruel fangs get you.

Oliver Routledge (11)
Whitburn School

A POEM DESCRIBING ME!

B   is for bold, bright, big and boastful
E   is for encourageable
N   is for naughty, needing, nosy
J   is for jealous
A   is for admiring, angry
M   is for minding, mindful
I   is for intelligent
N   is for nasty.

Ben Ball (12)
Whitburn School

MURDER

'A terrifying scream,
So I ran up to the bedroom'.
These were the words of the witness.
The detective explored an empty household,
With creaky doors and smashed-up breakfast bowls.
Suddenly the floorboards shook.
The detective shuddered.
The floor smashed,
He hung on,
In came a ghost,
It chuckled with anger.
It looked strangely familiar.
It struck the detective,
He let go with a scream.
It was the murder victim.

Lloyd Humphrey (11)
Whitburn School

THE CHILLER

Wind, wind everywhere
On the table, on the chair.

I wish that I was the wind
Going through the misty streets
Through the people's hair
As the dogs stare into thin air.

As the wind flies through the sky
The flags fly up high.

Kane Grant (11)
Whitburn School

ME

This is me:

I am as clever as a chimp,
But I am certainly not a wimp.

When I do get a fright,
I keep well out of sight.

I am as springy as a gazelle,
And I definitely do smell.

My sight is as good as an eagle
And I am as graceful as a seagull.

I am as beautiful as a ribbon tail,
And my claws are like sharp nails.

My hearing is acute,
But when I am born I am mute.

I have ears like a bat,
I am a cat!

Josh Gray (11)
Whitburn School

A MAGICAL WORLD

A biting breeze is blowing,
The snow is falling fast,
The darkness is quickly growing,
A snowy-white horse gallops past.

Nothing now is moving,
Everything seems dead.
The white blanket of snow is smoothing,
Something appears with eyes so red.

In fear, I ask myself, what is it?
Is it far? Is it near?
I jump over a tree which it hit.
I murmur, 'Is there another here?'

I can see the portal through which I came,
I begin to run, I'm almost back.
I jump through the hole, I've finished this 'game'
The portal disappears into an invisible crack.

Graeme Jones (11)
Whitburn School

MY DREAM PET

The pet I want won't fit a lead,
The pet I want is a giraffe called Reed.

The pet I want is big and strong,
The pet I want is a snake that's long.

The pet I want won't live in my house,
The pet I want is a grey grouse.

The pet I want can stand the snow,
The pet I want is a husky called Flo.

The pet I want is very frisky,
The pet I want is a dolphin named Whisky.

The pet I want won't sleep on my pillow,
The pet I want is a horse called Willow.

The pet I want I am unsure,
But I don't want one that lives in the sewer!

Rebecca Ross (12)
Whitburn School

Dad

What is a dad,
I wonder to myself?
Is it someone whose footsteps I will follow,
Whose leadership is their wealth?

Is it that he takes me
To all my football games,
Standing on the touchline
In sunshine, snow or rain?

Is it because he supports me,
Whatever I may do?
The encouragement he gives me
Continues through and through.

Is it because I'm special?
The attention he gives to me,
He always tries his very best,
Although he's as busy as could be.

Is it because I'm cared for,
No matter what I do?
My dad's irreplaceable
And I'll always love him too.

My dad is the best,
It's plain for all to see,
But what makes him number one
Is I know that he loves me.

Adam Shaw (12)
Whitburn School

THE TERROR OF TERRORISTS

As the plane took off, luggage packed,
Passengers were unaware they were being hijacked,
Many people on board, men and their wives,
Were taken hostage by men with knives.

These terrorists had taken over the plane,
Setting out to cause havoc and pain,
The first plane was steered into the North Tower,
At fifteen minutes to the hour.

As people looked on with fear in their eyes,
The second plane of terror came from the skies,
The plane circled round flying with power,
Crashing straight through the second tower.

Within an hour of such a devastating attack,
Down came the towers like dominoes stacked,
These magnificent buildings that once stood so tall,
Took only minutes to crumble and fall.

As the skies filled with dust and smoke,
People looked for loved ones filled with hope,
As the smoke cleared, all that was left was mess,
How many were dead? I would hate to guess.

This terrible act caused such a sad day,
For this crime people will pay,
Will America rest? Probably never,
But New York's skyline is changed forever.

Lee Brennan (13)
Whitburn School

TO LOVE OR TO CRY?

Why when I tell you I'm sorry,
Do you throw it back in my face?
When I tell you I never meant to hurt you,
You simply walk away.

When I tell you I need you,
Your expression says it all,
The story of child abuse was nationwide,
From the moment I could crawl.

Hitting, thumping, screeching, stabbing,
Things poor children have to face.
The torture, the pain, the misery
I feel is a huge disgrace!

The jeering, the mental torture,
Pains fly through the child.
Over time they become nothing,
The pain becomes mild!

I myself have nothing to fear,
My parents love me dearly,
Yet for so many children heartache is near,
It's vitally important, why can't you see?

So the next time you see child abuse,
Please don't turn a blind eye,
Each and every child, despite religion or race,
Is welcome to security and not to cry!

Kay Rooney (14)
Whitburn School

An Aquarian Dream

I see an Aquarian, Jennifer Claire,
With brown-coloured eyes and the same coloured hair.
You have a dream, Aquarius, I can tell,
Continue your studies and all will be well.

Your nature alone will quell any doubt
Of what your dream is all about.
As Venus enters into your chart,
I see a young woman with a kindly heart.

Not far in your future, I can see
Listening and sympathy are important to thee.
Your future, perhaps, will be in healthcare,
A compassionate nature you'll want to share.

Does physiotherapy sound right to thee?
I guess we will all have to wait and see.
Now I have given you a clue
Of what it is that you might do.

Peering into my crystal ball,
I do not see you alone at all.
Friends and family - there will always be,
Surrounded by love, is what I see.

With their support you can reach for your star.
Rise up Aquarius! It's not very far -
Have courage! Have faith! And you can say,
'I too have a dream to dream today!'

Jennifer Preston (14)
Whitburn School

ON THE STAGE

It's here,
The moment has arrived.
I feel sick,
I may throw up
All over the velvet.
The music starts,
I have to go on.
I feel as sick as a parrot.
I step on the stage,
What are my lines?
I open my mouth,
Nothing comes out.
Everybody's staring at me.
I open my mouth again,
The lines come out.
I run into the wings.
That is the feeling I get
When I go on stage.

Daryl Hall (11)
Whitburn School

MY NOGGIN

The thing inside my noggin
Helps when I'm confused
If I'm bored in class
It helps keep me amused

After a day at school
It is fully used
And if I have some homework
I think it's going to fuse

When it's finished a full day's work
It needs some rest at night
So it wakes up in the morning
Feeling sharp and bright.

Kevin Hodgson (12)
Whitburn School

TIGER, TIGER

Tiger, tiger, crouching low,
If they know he's there, away they go.
As he sneaks through the bush,
Not in a flurry or a rush,
He stalks his unexpecting prey,
He hopes it will be his lucky day.

It's very hot in the blistering sun,
He quickens his pace until it's a run.
This hungry tiger male,
Is determined not to fail.
He needs his meat for his lunch,
And when he catches them, their bones go crunch.

He quickly leaps out of the grass,
The deer disappears in a flash.
He might be able to catch some young deer,
The deer yelp and cry out in fear.

He never wonders how his prey feel,
Because he is too busy eating his meaty meal.
The tiger falls asleep on the floor,
Now everyone hopes he just won't *snore!*

Stephen Guthrie (11)
Whitburn School

MELODY FOR A BROKEN HEART

Who can tell us where we're going, why we think the way we do?
And what are the things that make me, me, the reasons you are you?
I'd reached a part of my journey that I never could have foreseen;
'I never thought I'd end up here,' I wept silently.

The music made me lift my head; I listened to the song,
I forgot my tears as I heard his voice, so clear, so proud, so strong.
Its beauty had no parallel, its emotions no disguise;
He came and sat beside me and he looked into my eyes.

He said, 'Do you believe in love beyond all doubt, beyond all fear?'
I closed my eyes, I closed my mind, pretending not to hear.
'I don't know what I believe anymore,' I finally replied,
'I was once only living so that I could love,
But something inside of me died.'

On his face I saw a smile that was filled with sorrow deep,
He said, 'Love is the question, love is the answer,
Love is the peaceful sleep.
Love is like the sunrise that brings light to the day,
Love is frost in January, gentle rain in May.'

'Love is pain,' I said to him, to which he disagreed,
'Love is overcoming pain and spite and lust and greed.
Love is stronger than them all and love will see you through,
To lose your faith in love would be to lose your faith in you.'

I lowered my head to dry my eyes, when I raised it he was gone,
But somewhere in the distance I could hear his magical song.
I thought about his lesson and I knew what I should do,
For through all the hurting, through all the lies,
Love will still remain true.

Lauren Ball (15)
Whitburn School

MR FINN

I sat alone at the back of my class,
Just watching the day go past.
When suddenly the door opened wide,
And an alien stepped inside.
The head teacher spoke up with a grin,
'This is your supply Mr Finn.'
His eyes, a million eyes in one,
His body reeked an awful pong!
'Silence now, books away!
You have no time to sit and play.'
He pointed a fat finger at Lucy How,
'Collect the class books in now!'
He walked over to the board,
And on it he wrote Martin Ford.
'That's detention Mr Ford.
Why? Because you're making me bored!'
His eyes grew big, his nostrils bigger,
His fingers and nails like mini diggers.
He wiggled and twitched,
Tickled and itched.
His sloppy mouth opened wide,
I would hate to mention what was inside.
A huge and smelly roar came gushing out,
This roar changed to a shout.
I couldn't see one bully standing up to him,
Not sir, Mr Finn.
The alien from outer space,
Who always bares a scary face.
So when we make an awful din,
The teacher just calls Mr Finn!

Nikita Mae Young (11)
Whitburn School

IT HAPPENS ALL OVER AGAIN

What was she to do?
He walked back into her fragile life,
Not a trace of hello,
No sign of a quick goodbye.
The things he felt for her,
The feelings were always there,
How could she not sense them?
Her mind filled with despair.

What should she say to him?
She was not sure in mind,
The pangs of love so strong
With her they did belong,
The blindness of her heart,
She did not feel his glare,
But she isolated life,
When should she stop and stare?

The final confrontation
Seemed to last too long.
She felt strangely awkward,
She still could not be strong.
He looked at her to say
He still loved her so.
Could she be the one
Who was still his beau?

Alice Barnes (14)
Whitburn School

THE EARTH

To me the Earth is big and round,
I like to listen to every sound.
The gas called wind that is high above,
Flutters around like a dove.
This thing we call Earth is hard to believe,
And still without trying we deceive.
This world that we live in, so fragile and precious
And all its beautiful animals, which we soon trap in meshes.
All of the creatures that run scared as they hide,
As we chase to see them and their beauty and pride.
This world that I live in is polluted and bare,
Of trees and crops that used to be there.
Concrete cities that blow out their waste,
Up and off to the air in space.
These concrete buildings, so ugly and bare,
I sometimes wish that they weren't there.
But then off goes our shops, McDonald's and more,
See that's typical of us, our modern galore.
This world that I live in, I want to renew,
This world that I live in, I want to pursue.
That as an individual I will change to stop
The pollution and debris that the ozone shall rot.
And soon it shall be perfect, shining with glee,
And soon it will show a new sense to see.
This world that I live in, so beautiful and strong,
This world that I live in is where I belong!

Hayley Conway (14)
Whitburn School

WHAT AM I?

I am fast as running,
But I don't like to run,
I am slow at swimming,
But I like to swim.

I am good,
Yet I am evil,
I am alive,
Yet I am dead.

I am thin,
Yet I am fat,
I am good at football,
But I don't like playing.

Reece Finch (11)
Whitburn School

MUSIC CLASS

When I am in music class
I sit and watch the clouds go past.
That's why I have a window seat,
To watch the farmer cut his wheat.
My teacher snaps his fingers
At the class singers,
I spot my name upon the board,
Detention for me, *oh Lord!*
Why punish me? I've done nothing wrong,
I was busy daydreaming and singing a song.
It's a music lesson, after all,
So why put me in detention hall?

Stephanie Urwin (12)
Whitburn School

SHOPLIFTING

I used to be a loner,
Very shy and lame,
But then I joined a gang of girls
Who lived on Brunswick Lane.

They all tried to be my friend and I was blinded by their niceness,
They said they'd help met to 'fit in',
But I was shocked to find
That these girls who seemed so nice, had shoplifting in mind.

The first time passed by so fast, I didn't even get caught,
After the second, third and fourth, it turned into an art,
But after the fifth, it dawned on me that I'd become addicted,
I'd better stop doing this now, I thought, or I may get lifted.

The sixth time came and I was going for the big one -
Stealing a crate of vodka
From the shop next door but one.
I entered the shop with drink on my mind,
But there on the bench was a wad of cash -
Could this have been more perfectly timed?

The next day I was watching the TV,
When there I was on 'Crimewatch',
I felt like a celebrity,
I mean, how many times do you see yourself labelled as *wanted*?

How could I have let this get out of hand?
I'd turn back time if I could.
I'd prefer to be 'Little Laura No Mates'
Than sitting in a cell.
I hate those girls who put me here,
I'll be seeing them in hell.

Laura Ferry (14)
Whitburn School

BAD BOY

'Goodnight,' said Mum and Dad,
'Today you've been very bad,
So to pay in return,
You'll be as scared as a worm,
When a human comes past to stare.'

There's a noise in your room,
You've just seen a broom
That's never been there before.
There's a noise under your bed,
That's going all around your head,
Get it away, out of the door.

I've been good in the past,
When I was very fast,
But now I am very slow.
As slow as a worm,
As slow as a snake,
As slow as I've ever been.

Laurie Slesser (11)
Whitburn School

BOYS, BOYS

Boys, boys, play with the ball,
Boys, boys are so tall.
Boys, boys in a gang,
Boys, boys make a bang.

Boys, boys are so down,
Boys, boys go to town.
Boys, boys, home again,
Boys, boys soon to be men.

Boys, boys are the best,
Boys, boys pass the test,
Boys, boys love to chat,
Boys, boys are not fat.

Boys, boys eat lots of food,
Boys, boys are in a mood.
Boys, boys at school,
Boys, boys jump in a pool.

Joe Harrison (11)
Whitburn School

Food

When I'm in a mood,
I always eat food.
Any kind will do.
When I'm in a mood,
I always eat food.
Watch out, I might eat you.
I will put you in a bun,
Yuma, yuma,
It will be fun.
When I'm in a mood,
I always eat food.
Pizza, chips,
More than that because that won't do.
When I'm in a mood,
I always eat food
And if you don't feed me, I'll get very rude,
But if you feed me, my mood will go.

Jack Blythe (11)
Whitburn School

The Goal

He takes a shot,
Everything is broken,
His mum goes mad,
Then he gets a poke.

He's sent outside,
Very upset,
Never to do it again,
It was his mum's favourite.

Sitting alone in the garden,
Thinking about what he's done,
Breaking his mum's vase,
A punishment needs to be done.

He washes, he scrubs,
He wipes, he cleans,
He cries, he screams,
He tries to flee.

And that's what happened to the boy
Who tried to score a goal.

Isra Gabal (11)
Whitburn School

The Winter Is Coming

The winter is coming
And the wind is blowing,
The snow falling,
The frost biting.

As the next day comes,
The snow's still falling
And Mum's calling.

Out in the snow,
A mum said, 'Are you wrapped up?'
'Of course,' said the child.

As the darkness came,
The snow still falling out
Of a dark blue sky,
People going in, probably with a cold or the flu.

Daniel Gollagly (11)
Whitburn School

THE HOUSE AT THE TOP OF THE HILL

Now if you have seen this house at night,
You'll be sure to get an awful fright.

Dust and mould here, broken glass there,
Silent rustles fill the air.

But in the sunlight, lo and behold,
A different story can be told.

The green, green grass glows in the day,
It is a lovely house, you could say.

The glossy paintwork all a-shine,
Happiness in the air, all the time.

Now you can see that this house is funny,
Because from the night, it turns sunny.

The house is creepy and dark at night,
But in daylight it is such a lovely sight.

The house at the top of the hill!

Stephanie McGuire (11)
Whitburn School

DOGS

A little dog is lots of hassle
When it chews the curtain tassel.
It will then move onto your gown,
Leaving you with a huge sad frown.
You could say it's going for a long walk,
But the children would scream instead of talk.

Then the slippers disappear,
The children's minds fill with fear.
Dad sits drinking beer,
Mum then screams, *'Oh dear, oh dear!'*
Dad then jumps
To see lots of lumps,
Then the carpet's ripped and torn
And, I think, the dog's just been born!

Gary Moon (11)
Whitburn School

AUTUMN WALK

As I walk through the streets the leaves I crunch,
As I walk through the fields the mud I squelch,
As I walk through the streets the smell of damp leaves fills the air,
As I walk through the fields rows of bare trees,
As I walk through the streets no one is there,
As I walk through the fields leaves fall down,
As I walk through the street the ground is brown with leaves,
As I walk through the fields the dew on the grass,
The smell of damp leaves and no one around,
Leaves cover ground, a crunch as you step,
Squelchy mud, this is my autumn walk.

Kieron McKay (11)
Whitburn School

WHY DOES LIFE HAVE TO END?

Waiting in a dark room,
Sitting all alone,
No one to talk to,
No one to phone.

Thinking of the old days,
Remembering people there,
Where have they gone now?
Why are they there?

Is it the sunshine that makes us come alive?
Do we still have memories, why do we survive?

Seeing people growing up,
Staring at the sky,
Waiting just for life to end.
Why do we have to die?

Rebecca Turner (12)
Whitburn School

SWEETS

Small, big, tall or wide
Dripping with sweetness from every side
Some you gobble and some you lick
Mars bars are definitely my favourite pick
Yum is what I always think
They come in different colours, even pink
Everyone likes them, who wouldn't?
To give them up I just couldn't
Sometimes sticky, sometimes sweet
You can even get some shaped like feet.

Verity Graham (11)
Whitburn School

ME MATE CALLED TED

When morning comes,
I raise my head,
I turn off the clock and get out of bed
And I always feed my spider, Ted.

As Ted got up that morning,
He said,
'I am dead,'
And that was the end of Ted.

As I saw Ted
In his bed,
I said,
'I really miss you, Ted.'

Ted was dead
In his bed
And so was
His brother, Ned.

Chris Glancey (11)
Whitburn School

MY JESS

They're large, they're small, they're yappy, they bark,
I love to take her to the park.
I see my friends walking by
As someone gives her a bit of pie.

She loves to run in the sun,
My Jess, she likes to have some fun.
I took her home to get a drink
Then she jumped up at the kitchen sink.

She saw the end of my dad's work coat,
She danced around like she was on a float.
She jumped in my dad's arms like a baby,
He closed her legs, for she is a lady.

Christa Archer (11)
Whitburn School

THE OLD MAN AND THE OLD HOUSE

There's an old house
Which is very cold
And there's an invitation in a fold,
Where there's writing very *bold*.

The man is old,
He's very bold,
He says he's cold,
But not cold,
He's . . .
Freezing cold.

3 months later . . .

The man is still cold
And is still very bold.
He always has pains
And gets called rude names.

3 months later . . .

The house is still cold
And has loads of mould.
The house is stacked with food,
Also there's graffiti, which is very rude.

Mark Hamblett (11)
Whitburn School

DAYS OF WAR

Shots echo round the trenches,
The soldiers know their fate.
Snipers are firing pot shots,
You see one hit your mate.

Back home in the cities,
Bombs are falling fast.
One hits round the corner,
You hope it is the last.

Spitfires are flying low,
Lancasters flying high,
Over in Germany bombs are dropping
Out of the dark, night sky.

On the shores of Normandy,
D-Day is taking place,
The landing crafts are swaying,
The Allies move to win the race.

In the skies of Britain,
A battle is taking place,
But the Spitfires are the one thing
That the Germans cannot face.

Robert Jones (11)
Whitburn School

IT WAS...

It was as pretty as a blooming flower,
It was as beautiful as the deep blue sea,
It was as handsome as a strong super hero,
Yes it was!

It was as gruesome as a dustbin's rag doll,
It was as ugly as an evil witch,
It was as monstrous as a sewer rat,
Yes it was!

Julie Whitfield (13)
Whitburn School

WHEN I FIRST STARTED SCHOOL

When I first started school
It was very cool,
Hanging out with friends
Will never end.

School dinners are always cold,
Sometimes they're never sold.
Dinner ladies are very scary,
So we have to be very wary.

People who bully are very naughty,
Especially my friend, Courtney.
She is always in detention,
That always is tension.

In lessons some people are naughty,
Especially my friend, Shorty,
He never shuts up.
All the girls think he's a cute pup.

The teachers are always giving homework,
It's always hard work.
Sometimes we watch videos,
It keeps us on our toes.

Nathan Potter (12)
Whitburn School

THE DENTIST

Sitting in the dentist's chair afraid,
Is it because I drank fizzy lemonade?
Sitting in the chair I feel ill,
The thought of the dentist's drill.

My body feels like it's chilling
As the dentist starts his drilling.
When he finishes he says, 'Have a drink,
Spit the water in the sink.'

He says, 'Open wide and I'll check the rest
To check your teeth are at their best.
Make another appointment, I'll see you soon,
Six months time, that will be in June.'

Sam Harwood (11)
Whitburn School

A FOOTBALL POEM

Eager bodies weave to and fro,
A tackle, a penalty,
Just two minutes to go.

Yes! Roar the crowds,
A long-awaited goal.
Was it Phillips? Was it Flo?
The commentator is sure to know.

Happy faces leave the ground,
A win at last.
1-0 at home,
What more could the fans ask?

Callum Watson (12)
Whitburn School

SUNDERLAND AFC POEM

We come up as champs, 105 points,
Can't wait to play Newcastle; must get 3 points.
Up the table we go, is this a dream?
At the Stadium of Light, we sure do gleam.
Top of the table, it can't last,
Just as I said, we finished 7th at the last.

Second season starts with a bang,
A win against Arsenal pleases the red and white gang.
On to Newcastle, can we beat them again?
Yes, Hutchinson scores; 2-1 my friend.
At 7th again, we just missed Europe,
Let's hope next season we don't get a hiccup.

Season 3 already, where are our signings?
A win against Ipswich, I hope our clouds still have silver linings.
Hutchinson leaves, what on Earth for?
Our performances really start to bore.
The season wears on and we're near relegation,
In comes Reyna, he can save our nation.
With a draw at Derby we're staying up,
Let's hope next season brings better luck.

We were promised big names,
But all we get are lames.
The season starts, we bore the crowd.
No score at Blackburn, here comes the black cloud.
At the last minute, we get Stewart and Flo,
Can Sunderland turn it around and put on a show?
Against Newcastle, we lost 2-0,
Peter Reid's time is running thin.
Come on Sunderland, start to try,
Oh, and by the way, I'm *Sunderland till I die!*

Luke Golding (13)
Whitburn School

SUICIDE

I can't believe she did it.
My best friend died yesterday,
It was suicide.
Why didn't she talk to me?

She said she needed to get away, escape,
I can't believe it.
2 days ago, we were shopping,
Everything was fine, until now.

I want to see her so much,
To talk to her,
Tell her that everything is going to be OK,
I know I can't do this anymore.

There are so many people that care about her,
Yet she still thinks her life is not worth living.
What about her parents, brothers, family?
What about me?

It's not the same without you here,
Sure, I have other friends,
But they're not you.
They could never be you.

She took an overdose,
Found some pills in her cupboard,
Thought, *what the hell?*
2 hours later she was found.

They rushed her to hospital,
But it was too late,
She was gone.
I still can't believe it.

I miss her.

Emma Mossavi (13)
Whitburn School

STAY AWAY

'Come on, let's try it,' a young girl says to her friend.
'It'll be fun! Something new, exciting!
There's nothing to it
And you know you won't regret it!'

So they pop their pills, preparing for 'fun',
The people around doing the same.
Soon they're screaming, laughing,
Such a great time, but it doesn't last.

As their high starts to dip, they don't want it to end,
Don't want to leave their fantasy world,
So a few more pills they quickly down,
Awaiting another dose of fun.

But the fun is finished, over,
As one doesn't feel too well
And to the floor she falls
As the other watches, confused, alone.

The flashing lights, the deafening noise
All becoming reality . . .

Well those girls were us
And now she's gone.
Why was I stupid enough to lose my senses?
She's suffered, because of me.

Now I know first hand,
Drugs kill, drugs cause suffering,
I must warn others
To stay away.

I miss her.

Emily Shields (13)
Whitburn School

CARS

There are all kinds of cars,
Cars for all kinds of people.
Jaguars, Multiplas, Puntos and Beetles.

Some cars are small,
Some cars are large,
Some are kept in the street,
Some in the garage.

There are various colours,
Such as black, green or gold,
Some delicate,
Some very bold.

If asked for my favourite,
I would readily say
The Maclaren F1 is
The best car today.

Thomas Crutwell (12)
Whitburn School

GOLDEN TIGER

Golden tiger swift and sly,
Catches prey with a blink of an eye,
Creeping through deep green grass,
Eyes sparkling like silver glass,

Golden like the setting sun,
Catching prey is really fun,

I wonder how you got this way,
Golden tiger with a silver sway.

Daniel Pye (12)
Whitburn School

SUPERMARKET

Supermarkets are very big,
Children shouting, playing tig.

Aisles full of drinks and cans,
Selling objects like pots and pans.

Fridges full of frozen food,
Children screaming being rude.

Tops, trousers, shoes and jeans,
People buying tins of beans.

People buying things like pills,
And queuing up at the tills.

Now they are leaving to the car park,
Time to go home it's getting dark.

Helen Thornton (12)
Whitburn School

TENNIS

Hitting the ball over the net
Moving across the court
People making different bets
And young people being taught.

Shaking the hand of the other player
Talking to the very old mayor
Going out into the car
People shouting, 'You're great.'

He falls down on the floor
Shouting, 'Yes, yes I have won!'
He feels great and very happy.

Chris Kear (11)
Whitburn School

ODE TO SIR BOBBY

Sunderland, Newcastle
The Tyne & Wear derby
Sounds like hassle
Best call in the Toon army

Beer flowing, people screaming
Mud flying, colours streaming
Given saves the shot by inches
Bobby shouts while the whole crowd flinches

The whistle blows stadium explodes
A win for Newcastle 2-0
The crowd is aghast admits the thrill
The tears, the anguish the anticipation
And it all depended on the formation.

Daniel Callan (12)
Whitburn School

AN EMERALD IS AS GREEN AS GRASS

Clouds are as big as a comprehensive school
Clouds are as soft as a baby's bum
Clouds are as white as the cold snow
Clouds are as cold as the slippy ice
Clouds are as pretty as the beautiful princess
Clouds are as small as a bouncy ball
Clouds are as tough as a wall
Clouds are as high as Mount Everest
Clouds are as bright as the sun
Clouds are as shaped like an animal
Clouds are as fluffy as cotton wool
Clouds are as smooth as a teddy bear.

Louise Bailey (13)
Whitburn School

THE BOY

The boy is an incredible thing,
He eats stuff like lime and ming.
Never more, never less,
The boy is just more of a pest.
What I know he eats something different,
Scrambled egg or toast.
He is not eating anything because he has just seen a ghost.
Wakes up next morning
Rubbing his eyes and yawning
Asked for breakfast,
Just the same but mixed with chocolate and peanut.
Has the boy changed his appetite?
Well we say he is incredible
But what we know still lies beneath!

Antony Dorothy (12)
Whitburn School

A POEM ABOUT THE SECOND WORLD WAR

Boom, boom, the guns are firing
The German leader's off his rocker
He's dropping bombs like the raindrops
Because he's raving mad.

Winston Churchill is a winner
Adolf Hitler is a loser
Why did he start this crazy war?
We know he's going to lose!

The Nazi army is getting thrashed
Mr Hitler knew he would lose
So why did he start the war?

Alex Nicol (11)
Whitburn School

THE SANDS OF LIFE

Cold. Cold a day as I have ever seen,
Almost as cold as my rifle felt in my hands.
The whirring of the boat's engine the only sound on the air,
Even as the planes flew past, in the direction of the sands.

Land. The sudden realisation as it loomed into view,
That all the souls surrounding me, bound to the same fate,
Were aware that what they saw before them
Lay Hell, and we were a the gate.

Bullets. The first few soldiers stepped off the boat,
Only to drop back down again like flies.
I scrambled my way over the side of the boat,
To feel the icy cold water stabbing me like knives.

Death. All around me my eyes fell upon death.
The screaming came through many shapes and forms.
Some were from the mortar shells rearing through the sky,
Most were from the men, whom I had no time to mourn.

Darkness. I could feel the life drain from me
As the .50 calibre bullets coursed through me.
Time stopped and all my pain disappeared,
I caught the faint, fading sound of crashing waves on the sea.

Rising up to the gates of Heaven,
To Saint Peter I shall tell,
'One more soldier reporting, sir -
I have served my time in Hell.'

Chris Furness (14)
Whitburn School

MY PERFECT LUNCH

I hate coffee,
But boy I love toffee.
I like bran flakes,
But I guess I prefer pancakes.
It is true I love peas,
But even more so cheese.
I do like beans,
But I really, really like my greens.

I hate cherries,
But boy I love berries.
I like lemon,
But I guess I prefer melon.
It is true I like prawn,
But even more so corn.
I do like sprout,
But I really, really like trout.

I hate Spam,
But boy I love ham.
I like wheat,
But I guess I prefer meat.
It is true I like chips,
But even more so in dips.
I do like spices,
But I really, really like rices.

This would make my perfect lunch.

Craig Todd (12)
Whitburn School

AMERICAN FOOTBALL

The Barbarians run across the pitch
Trying to score that important touchdown,
6 points you shall get and another 1
If you kick it through the posts.

The crazy men charging for the brown-striped ball,
So someone's going to get hurt.
Oh no, someone has been throwing through a hall
And has just ripped his shirt.

American football is a teamwork game,
To win a match you need to be insane,
Because it is a man's game.

To be a good quarter-back, try to get obese
And if you come to watch the match, always bring a fleece.
When you try to get obese, try not to fall on Papa Smurf
When he's playing on the turf.

Michael Brookes (12)
Whitburn School

FACE THE PACE

I love running in a race,
But it's always one big chase.
I think it's really fun,
But watch out for that firing gun.

You can always run,
In the red-hot blazing sun,
But it's actually the same,
In the pouring rain.

It doesn't matter if you win or lose,
It might just be you're wearing the wrong running shoes,
So even if you lose and you're bruised,
Don't go down in them horrible blues.

Bethany Hammonds (11)
Whitburn School

D-DAY

Splash, splash,
The sound of water against the boat.
Splash, splash,
Slowly getting closer to shore.

I can hear gunfire,
I can hear screams,
I try not to think
About what lies ahead.

As I get out of the boat,
I can see dead bodies.
The smell of sweat
And blood is in the air.

In the sea of red
Lie a few of our men
Who have been killed in battle
By the enemy we fear.

We make our way
Slowly up the beach,
Heading towards the hills
Where a living hell awaits . . .

Graham Burn (13)
Whitburn School

THE SEASONS

The bulbs start peeping through the ground
The birds start singing their wonderful sound
The leaves begin to grow on the trees
The cold north wind is now a breeze
It's spring

Flowers are blooming, their colours are bright
Children are playing out late at night
Birds are nesting high up in the trees
It's the season for wasps and bees
It's summer

Leaves are beginning to drop from the trees
Say goodbye to summer's warm breeze
Children are snuggling up warm in bed
Outside their cheeks are rosy-red
It's autumn

Snow is falling upon the ground
Snowmen being built are short and round
Icicles are hanging from the trees
Ponds and rivers begin to freeze
It's winter.

***Daniel Fishwick (11)
Whitburn School***

HORRORS IN THE NIGHT

I woke up in the night,
Scared, frightened.

Shadows floating all around me,
Yet not a movement in the air.

As silence glooms all around me,
I feel the shivers shooting up my spine.

I see figures in the dark,
They scare me, every night.

I was only four when I saw them first,
I'm thirteen now, I think I'm cursed.

Will I ever recover from my awful frights,
Or will they haunt me every night?

Claire Robson (13)
Whitburn School

ANGEL OF THE NORTH

I stand in Gateshead
On a large grassy hill,
I am 65 feet tall,
My wings spread 175 feet wide.

Thousands of people come and go,
To observe me
As if I was an object from outer space.

I stand all day, strong,
Like a soldier in battle,
Through all the weather and seasons,
I stand untouched.

I am a rusty-brown colour
And can be seen from many miles away.
I have no heart and no emotions,
Just a large chest of rusty steel.

I will stand here for
Days, months, years, even decades,
But I will continue to be myself,
I am the Angel Of The North!

Sarah Nicholson (13)
Whitburn School

My Time Has Come

Slowly, steadily up I climb,
Soon it will be my last time.

Up on the platform there is a good view,
A terrifying final memory too.

I see my mother in the crowd
And hear her weeping out aloud.

I wish I could spare her the horror
Of her only son's departure.

A chamber pot is emptied out of a window,
Showering urine on my to-be widow.

Alas there is an itch in my neck,
I wish my hands were untied for a sec.

The executioner appears from the crowd,
As everyone roared amazingly loud.

Slowly I pull off my old coat,
As the rope slipped around my throat.

The lever is pulled,
The trapdoor dropped.

There is a sickening crack,
Above my back.

My body feels like lead,
Thoughts rush through my head.

My legs feel numb,
My time has come.

Goodbye cruel twist of fate,
'Tis you I truly, truly hate.

Arrgghh! It's that, I must go,
My spirit is very low.

Arrgghh! Good-goodbye,
Goodbye cruel *wor-aieee!*

Matthew Woodhouse (11)
Whitburn School

LIGHT

Light is needed all around,
In many places can it be found.
Its uses are many and many at that,
With a click of a switch it's all around.

Light can be found in most every place,
It brightens up the darkest space.
With a click of a switch,
Or a twist of a torch,
Brings light of almost any sort.

Some lights are on all the time,
Some lights are on a timer,
Some lights get switched on manually,
But all lights help in some way.

Lights can't be touched,
Lights can't be smelt,
But light is helpful,
When it is dark.

It shines and brightens up the day,
Bringing freshness and brightness,
Putting the darkness away.

Steven Rutter (13)
Whitburn School

Urban War

Above the clouds,
Looking down,
I have to jump,
But how?

Momentarily,
My friends are behind me,
And soon we shall see,
Our unknown enemy.

I suck in my gut
And swallow my fear,
I take a few steps forward,
And all through the air.

A few seconds later,
I pull my ripcord,
And breathe a sigh of relief,
As it slows my huge fall.

In sight of the town square,
Could our enemy be there?
I can't keep a lid on my fear
And a chill goes up my spine from my toes to my hair.

We hit the ground,
With a large, painful thud,
Some flee under the stress,
And I wish I could.

I join up with my squad,
And hide behind a wall,
Shots rebound off it,
And bricks and cement fall.

So this is urban war,
A sight I wish I hadn't saw.

Sean Wakefield (13)
Whitburn School

MY LIFE POEM

Walking through this autumn path,
On my way to the aftermath,
Years of pain these eyes have seen,
Trying to retrace the places I've been,

Hoping to take one step back,
To put my life back on track,
To avoid the battles that I had fought,
To find the happiness that I had sought,

Along this autumn path I walk,
Along this autumn path I walk,
On my way to the aftermath,
Please make sure
You don't take my path.

Cameron Walker (14)
Whitburn School

MY SISTER AND I

Each night we lie,
My sister and I.
We dream of what we'll do.
Tomorrow we'll rise
With the birds in the skies
And play 'til the day is through.

We're never apart,
Lizzy stays in my heart,
I love my sister so.
We can play every day,
I want her to stay,
I'll never let her go.

Each night we lie,
My sister and I,
We dream of what we'll do,
Tomorrow we'll rise
With the birds in the skies
And play 'til the day is through.

We could play hide-and-seek,
A new game every week
Or maybe something new.
My sister is great,
I cannot wait
Until the night is through.

Emma Irvine (11)
Whitburn School

THE ORPHAN

Sitting in this musky damp
The stench invades my nose
With a pool of disembodied liquid at my feet
My youth is captivated by loneliness.

Eternity is lost in my thoughts
As I dwindle over my purpose
This putrid excuse of a child
Who doesn't deserve a family.

Here I sit in my decaying corner
Cringing from the parasites
Hiding from the pain
Forbidden from the outside society

Sleeping on the floor
With my loneliness as my blanket
Where will I go after the long sleep?
It must be better!

I can see the world
The love of others
I can see my corner
That holds my misery

I have seen my life
And I am an orphan.

Zoe Muse (14)
Whitburn School

CHOCOLATE BOB

Chocolate Bob
He lives down Strawberry Lane
He is a bit mad
But that ain't bad

Bob, Bob, Chocolate Bob
His best friend is a doorknob

Chocolate Bob
He worships turnips
He works in toil
And is not safe to boil

Bob, Bob, Chocolate Bob
He is not a slob

Chocolate Bob
Well that's him for you
If you ever see him
Just don't call him Rob.

Jamie Anderson (11)
Whitburn School

ANIMALS

Big, fat, podgy and round
Making lots of weird sounds
Chewing, snarling, hissing, clawing
They do this when they're not snoring.

Black, white, ginger and brown
When they're sad they always frown
Feet, claws, fangs and wings
It's amazing what nature brings.

Birds lay their eggs in their nests
They also eat our garden pests
Bees fly around pollinating flowers
But that's only when there's no showers.

Butterflies flutter when their wings have hardened
And fly around all the pretty gardens
But that's when they're not in my tummy
Cos when I'm nervous, *it's really not funny!*

Jonathon McCulley (11)
Whitburn School

FOOTBALL

I can hear the noise
As I start to run.
We warm up on the pitch
Oh heck! It's only fun.

We kick off to 'Hooray,' 'Come on.'
Me in defence, my mate up front
They receive the ball in midfield
And give it a punt.

I collect the ball
To a swarm of cheers
I aim to shoot
The goalie clears.

We get the ball yet again
My boots feel like coal
Our attacker shoots
What a goal!

Christopher James Gardner (11)
Whitburn School

CLOUDS

Clouds are as soft as candyfloss
And as white as snow
They'll change to different shapes
Wherever you go

Sometimes they are as pretty as a picture
Or as dark as the night
They can be as big as a house
As small as a mouse
As high as the sky
As low as my toe

Clouds can be as fast as the wind
Racing like a speeding car
Or as still as a statue
Looking for a star

Clouds can be as light as a feather
As fluffy as a chick
Or
They can be full of rain
Which is a real pain!

Vicki Midlane (13)
Whitburn School

THE ZOO

The zoo is full of fun
Children laugh and run
Animals make loads of noise
While management chase naughty boys

Lions run and pant
While anteaters eat an ant
Giraffes eat out of trees
In cages live flees and bees

Worms and ants all live in mud
Listen to children who say you should
Come along for a great time,
And if you're lucky stand in some animal slime

Animals and tigers, elephants too
Have a good time down at the zoo
There's crocodiles and parrots so come along,
To the one place that children belong.

Emmy Campbell (11)
Whitburn School

ME, MYSELF AND I

I have a brain as big as a medium tennis ball,
But yet it is not as clever.

I have a part of beauty in life,
But will never be ugly, never ever.

I like to have happiness,
But not when I'm fighting.

I like to have noise,
But I also like to have peace.

I like to have freedom,
But I like to have time by myself.

I have lots of courage,
But not enough to climb a mountain.

I have got patience,
But not when I'm tired.

I like to be loved,
But not when I'm bad.

Lauren Jackson (11)
Whitburn School

THE FINAL CUP ROUND

This is a ball
That got kicked by the boot.

This is a ball
That got kicked by the boot
that made the ball fly across the back garden.

This is a ball
That got kicked by the boot
That made the ball fly across the back garden
That scored the winning goal.

This is a ball
That got kicked by the boot
That made the ball fly across the back garden
That scored the winning goal
That flew over the fence.

This is a ball
That got kicked by the boot
That made the ball fly across the back garden
That scored the winning goal
That flew over the fence
That broke the window.

This is the hand
That hit the back of the goal scorer.

This is the hand
That hit the back of the goal scorer
That made the boy cry.

This is the hand
That hit the back of the goal scorer
That made the boy cry
But at least he won the Cup.

Anthony Dunn (12)
Whitburn School

THE BLACK CAT

As the black cat walked mysteriously up the hill,
His fur as black as coal ready to kill,
His glowing green eyes,
His miaows sounding like sighs.

His paws walking along the icy cold ground,
His ears are pricked up for any sudden sound,
Making no sound as silent as can be,
As quiet as the gentle waves flowing in the sea.

As this cat is so lonesome and stray
He wishes for a home with a fire to lay.
As he sleeps he dreams of a boy
Who has given him a home with his heart full of joy.

As he wakes he stretches and yawns
Full of expectations as a new day dawns.
Away in the distance a small tweeting sound,
As he creeps over, a small robin is found.

Tweeting, chirping and pecking the cat's paws,
'Follow me, follow me, to a house with a wooden door.'
So he stretched out his paws and began to run
The small robin flies thinking, *this is quite fun.*

Two minutes later he stands before the door
But as he thinks for a moment and looks at his paw,
There is a small boy, who plays with his toys,
He has found him and purrs, joy of joys.

The robin has flown off thinking, my work is done here
And goes off to solve more problems that are near.
The cat has found an owner and a perfect home to stay,
With a big warm fire and a soft bed to lay.

Never say dreams can't come true!

Amy Overton (11)
Whitburn School

THE OTHER WORLD

War is but a cry away
Will Third World countries see another day?
Why do people want to cause such pain?
Is it so they look good? Is it really all in vain?

We take the world around us all for granted
The way we see the world really is slanted
We worry about clothes and make-up
Some people only have rags,
I wonder if they have even heard of make-up?

We are all materialistic
Let's try to be a bit more realistic
We don't worry about hunger
Lots of people are well past hunger

Illness is all around
Will ever a cure be found?
Just stop this suffering
Will the smog of illness ever stop smothering?

All these innocent lives are being taken
God please be a bit more forsaken
Give the victims of war, illness and suffering the happiness
                                        they deserve
Keep all the suffering in reserve

Let's all work together
Let's help the future forever
To stop war, suffering and the people who cause it
This may be the cure, this may be it!

Lauren Wilkinson (13)
Whitburn School

IT'S A LONG AND COMPLICATED PATH

It's a long and complicated path,
But every person born into this world
Has to walk it.
It's a long and complicated path,
But you, yes you
Have to travel it.

It's a long and complicated path,
Full of twists and turns,
Obstacles and hurdles.
It's a long and complicated path,
Surrounded by thorns and hedges
Spears and spikes.

It's a long and complicated path,
We have no option but to follow it
Till it ends.
It's a long and complicated path,
No way out,
No stopping.

It's a long and complicated path,
Winding like silver
Along a river bank
It's a long and complicated path,
Those who don't walk it,
Don't live!

It's a long and complicated path,
Life!

Laura Handy (14)
Whitburn School

WILD WRONG ANIMALS FROM A ZOO

I once went to a big zoo,
I didn't know what to do.
Then all of a sudden I heard a rage,
Coming from the corner in a cage.
In the cage was a Brazilian baboon
And by its side was a Cuban cocoon.

I then looked to my right
And got a terrible fright.
There in front of me beside the wall,
A long-necked creature, twenty feet tall.
I then realised it was a German giraffe,
Like the Hawaiian hyenas it started to laugh.
Some Chinese cats with fur in tats, were chasing around the
                                                    Russian rats.

In another part of the zoo,
Was some African apes too.
An African ape
Had done its best to escape.
It ran around the land
And then was tired and fell asleep on the sand.
There was also a lot of Welsh weasels,
Who badly caught the measles.
A Slovakian snake
Had the shakes.
It took a pill,
Because the vet said it was ill.

The Turkish tigers were friends with an English elephant,
Which I thought was brilliant!
The time I had at the zoo was great
And would go again on another date.

Anna Carter (11)
Whitburn School

IN THE MOONLIGHT

In the moonlight,
I stand alone, tonight,
The stars are out so bright,
Shining on, giving light.

I'm so glad, standing here,
Even though I'm alone I have no fear,
No worries and no battles to fight,
Just staring out at the wonderful sight.

Unlike some who have no food tonight,
They're starving while I'm staring at the stars, so bright,
People dying while I'm having fun,
Some slaving away in the heat of the sun.

It's so hot in the place where they are,
If we want to get there we have to travel very far,
They have no time to enjoy the weather,
They have no fun they have no pleasure.

While I'm standing here in the moonlight,
Staring at the stars so bright,
I have so much to give,
I could help them live.

Just think tonight, in your warm bed,
What could you do? They would be happy with some bread,
You could help them survive another day,
With just a small part of your pay.

In the red-hot sun to live, they must fight,
While I stand alone, in the moonlight.

Laura Wilkinson (13)
Whitburn School

POPPY

My dog Poppy
Is very sloppy
She slops her food
On the floor
And then she
Barks for more
She spills her water
On the mat
Then she chases
Next door's cat
Over the fence
She climbs and jumps
And sometimes she does
Smelly pumps
But I love Poppy
And that's a fact
And nowt will ever
Change that!

Stefanie Ford (11)
Whitburn School

WHAT IS THE POINT?

Soldiers are a bit mad.
All they do is shoot each other
And when the war is over, the winner always helps the loser.
What is the point?

War is a bit crazy.
All people want is power.
One man can cry from the verge of insanity,
What is the point?

Soldiers are a bit pointless.
They spend all their time training,
For what? Getting shot!
What is the point?

Craig Young (11)
Whitburn School

THE OBJECT COLLECTOR

A man came this morning
Dressed in black and white
I opened the door while yawning
I got such a fright.

He took away the pots
He took away the cans
He took away the TV
He took away the pans.

He took away the table
He took away the door
He took away the pictures
He took away the floor.

He took away the window
He took away the chairs
He took away the books
He took away my bears!

A man came this morning
Dressed in black and white
He took away my objects
It was such a sight.

Vanessa Curry (12)
Whitburn School

THE EAGLE

As he swoops down over the rocky cliff,
His golden feathers glisten in the sunlight,
These beautiful creatures are a myth,
I never knew a creature could look like this.

Diving, diving, down he goes,
Where he's going to land, no one knows.
He catches his prey
And back up he goes.

Sitting there on his perch,
Way up there, miles above the Earth,
He now stands up straight and tall,
The animals below look very small.

Now his day has come to an end,
His luxurious life he must now bend,
Now the winter days have come
And the fierce winds again start to blow.

Now he waits for the precious spring
And the new life it shall bring.
Every night he shall mourn
For the new day and the dawn.

Andrew Clark (11)
Whitburn School

SPORT

I like playing football,
Athletics too.
I don't enjoy losing,
But what can I do.
Whatever the outcome,
I try my best,
It's a pity we aren't as good as the rest.

I may be the greatest footballer yet,
Dribbling and heading straight into the net
My legs are bruised and my body is battered,
It all felt great before I got clattered.
I powered the ball towards the goal,
It flew through the air with such curl,
I'm fed up with all friends saying I play like a girl!

Johnathon Tulip (14)
Whitburn School

SPIDERS

Lurking in the garden,
Hiding in the darkness,
Lying there,
Hiding there,
Waiting for you.

There are millions of spiders,
They mainly live down under,
They're always getting poked with sticks,
That's why they hide, no wonder.

Lurking in the garden,
Hiding in the darkness,
Lying there,
Hiding there,
Waiting for you.

Big spiders, small spiders,
They're all the same in a way.
They've all got eight long, spindly legs,
And only want to play!

Sam Keane (11)
Whitburn School

THE START OF SCHOOL

School is alright,
I am very bright.
My friends think I am a fool,
But that is cool.

The presentation of work is important,
But the detentions are unimportant.
The merits are crucial
But the teachers are rueful.
PE is cool
Because the teachers sometimes act like fools.
Dinner time is good,
But the dinners taste like mud.

The lessons are fun,
But the children sometimes run.
My friends are always wrong,
Especially my friend Wong.

Jamie Harding (12)
Whitburn School

STORMY

The firelight flickers
As the lightning flashes,
The clouds blackout the sky
And the thunder clashes.

The rooms light up
In all different shades,
As night-time comes
And daylight fades.

Suddenly there's a bang
It's the thunder rumbling
And once again
The lightning comes tumbling.

Laura Fielding (11)
Whitburn School

THROUGH MY MIRROR

Maybe through my mirror
There's a whole new world to see,
Maybe there's another girl
Who looks the same as me.

Maybe she's annoyed at me
For making her move backwards,
Or maybe that's the norm for her
And I'm not moving onwards.

Maybe I'm not the one in control,
As I've always thought to be.
Perhaps I am a mere reflection
Of the world that she can see.

Maybe the seasons I've grown to know,
Spring, summer, winter, fall,
Aren't really there at all.
They're just a reflection on her wall.

Maybe I haven't just written this poem,
Maybe these ideas aren't mine.
Maybe she's sitting at her desk right now,
Thinking of a word to rhyme.

Faye Buckingham (13)
Whitburn School

THE PLAYGROUND

School bell rings,
Ting-a-ling,
All out,
Running around,
Stomp, stomp,
Everyone shouting,
Screaming with laughter,
Also tears,
School bell rings,
Ting-a-ling,
All in,
Back to work,
Let's begin.

Victoria White (12)
Whitburn School

SHARKS

The silent predator slides through the water
Like jelly on a plate,
Cutting shoals of fish in half as it swims.

The swift hunter travels quickly through the reef,
Like a torpedo aimed at a ship,
Looking for food as it bolts along the ocean bed.

The streamlined pursuer darts diagonally across the ocean
At his unwary prey.
A small splash occurs at the surface and the seal is no more at bay.
The seal's parents are in dismay,
But the great white shark survives to fight another day.

Michael Gowland (11)
Whitburn School